GOOD HOUSEKEEPING
How to Remove Stains

~plus general care and repair

D0011951

EBURY PRESS

LONDON

Published in Great Britain by Ebury Press
National Magazine House, 72 Broadwick Street,
London WIV 2BP

First impression 1979
Second impression 1979

ISBN 0 85223 106 7

Research: Gillian Smedley
Text: Cassandra Kent
Designer: Derek Morrison
Cartoons: Robert Broomfield

Photoset by Typesetting Services Ltd, Glasgow
Printed by The Anchor Press Ltd, Tiptree, Essex
Bound by William Brendon and Son Ltd, Tiptree, Essex

Contents

Acknowledgements

We wish to thank the following organizations for their help in compiling this book.

BAYER FIBRES (UK) LTD
THE BOOTS COMPANY LTD
BRICK DEVELOPMENT ASSOCIATION
BRITISH CARPET MANUFACTURERS'
  ASSOCIATION
BRITISH MAN-MADE FIBRES FEDERATION
COURTAULDS LTD
THE FABRIC CARE RESEARCH ASSOCIATION
FURNITURE INDUSTRY RESEARCH ASSOCIATION
HOME LAUNDERING CONSULTATIVE COUNCIL
ICI FIBRES
INTERNATIONAL WOOL SECRETARIAT
LEVER BROTHERS LTD
THE JOHN LEWIS PARTNERSHIP
OPTICAL INFORMATION COUNCIL
PROCTER & GAMBLE LTD
VICTORIA AND ALBERT MUSEUM

Metric measurements

In accordance with metric development, spoon measurements in this book are given in millilitres. If you do not have a set of metric measuring spoons the conversion is as follows:

1 teaspoon	5 ml
1 tablespoon	15 ml

Warning

Many stain removing agents, including proprietary products, are potentially harmful if not actually poisonous. Some are highly flammable; others give off toxic fumes.

The sensible course is to treat all stain removing substances with caution and in the case of proprietary products, go by the manufacturers' directions scrupulously. Follow these simple rules as a routine measure.

When using:
Always work in a well-ventilated room, preferably with the window open. Never use stain removing agents in a room where there is a naked flame, pilot light or radiant heater. Never smoke while working with, or anywhere near to, stain removing agents.
Do not decant the solvent into another container.
Wear rubber gloves.

When storing:
Keep all the items in your stain removing kit out of the reach of children or elderly people whose sight is failing, or who may become confused; best of all, keep your kit locked away.
Never put away anything that is not clearly labelled.
Store—and indeed buy—small quantities only of all stain removing substances.

Take extra precautions when using or handling:

Methylated spirit	Highly flammable and poisonous
Spirits of salts	Poisonous and corrosive
Amyl acetate	
Liquid lighter fuel	
Turpentine	
White spirit, or turpentine substitute	Flammable and dangerous to inhale; poisonous
Non-oily nail varnish remover	
Cellulose thinners	
Ammonia	Unpleasant fumes; avoid contact with eyes, skin or clothing; poisonous

How to Use this Book

Part 1 : *Types of Stain—and the Solvent to Use,* gives you essential background information on stain removal, together with details of useful items to include in your stain removal kit.

To deal with a particular stain—say, cod liver oil—turn to Part 2 : *A–Z of Stain Removal,* and look up COD LIVER OIL. Under this entry you will find a number of sub-headings, from 'on carpets' to 'on table linen', telling you exactly what to do.

If, however, your problem is one of general cleaning and care (say, your sisal matting is looking grubby, or you'd like advice on caring for a tortoiseshell-backed hair brush) turn to Part 3 : *Surfaces—and how to care for them.* You will find the answer under SISAL MATTING or TORTOISESHELL.

For burns, dents, scratches, *etc* on furniture, again see Part 3, under FURNITURE.

1

Types of Stain - and the Solvent to Use

Spills occur in even the best-run homes—and they're not just caused by high-spirited children or bouncy pets knocking over flower vases. Everyone has 'off' days when they drop things—an unexpected noise can cause an otherwise steady hand to falter, a minute's delay can mean a burn mark on a saucepan. Then there are the stains that creep up on a home unaided by human hand. Things like mildew on shower curtains or leather-bound books, fly specks on fabric lampshades and soot marks on brickwork.

However, with a little knowledge, speed and care, most stains *can* be removed—often leaving no trace and almost always producing a distinct improvement on the stain mark itself. In this book we tell you how to deal with (almost) all household stains yourself from both the point of view of the stains *and* the surfaces on which they occur. So whether you've spilled an entire bottle of ink on your best rug or bought a house where the carpets look as if unmentionable deeds have been perpetrated on them, read on.

In Part 1 we deal with general stain lore and suggest how to build up your own stain removal kit. Part 2 lists stains alphabetically and is for you to turn to in emergencies when you know what's been spilled. Part 3 lists various household surfaces and items, again alphabetically, and tells you how to care for them on a regular basis to keep them in good condition.

General points on stain removal

As a general rule, it's much easier to remove any stain if you *treat it as soon as it occurs* or, at any rate, as soon as you realize it's occurred. The occasion when you shouldn't do this is when the particular stain, or surface on which it has fallen, requires professional treatment. We tell you when it's safe to do it yourself or when you should get professional help.

Before treating any stain you must consider three things: the stain itself, the surface on which it is, and any special dye, treatment or finish on that surface. It is essential, whatever method of removal you adopt—be it cold water or a proprietary cleaner—to *test it first* on a small, hidden area of the surface. This need take no more than a minute or so and could prevent you ruining something irrevocably. Even if you're sure that you know what product gets what stain out of what surface, it may be that there is some additional unknown factor present in what you are treating, so a test run is vital.

There are a number of quick first-aid treatments which can be applied to certain things and are useful if, for example, you are in mid-dinner party or meeting and don't feel able to stop and administer thorough stain removal treatment on the spot. Non-greasy stains can be sponged or rinsed through with cold water. Greasy ones can be sprinkled with talcum powder to stop them spreading. On tablecloths, salt thrown on to wine, fruit or beetroot stains will stop them spreading. Salt should *not* be thrown on to carpets as it tends to affect colours and to leave a damp patch which will attract moisture and make it soil more readily.

One golden rule is to *go cautiously* when treating stains. Milder methods repeated as often as necessary are far more effective than a blast from a strong solvent which is more likely to damage the surface than to get out the stain.

Bear in mind that a stain has fallen *on* to something and therefore needs to be taken *off* it. When applying a solvent to an absorbed stain (*see* STAINS DEFINED) that hasn't responded to sponging or laundering, work from the side underneath the stain, holding a dry, white absorbent pad on the other side. A built-up stain (*see* STAINS DEFINED) should, where possible, be treated from the underside with a pad held on top of the mark so that the deposit is not driven through the fabric. Any absorbent pad used in these ways should be moved around continually to prevent any of the stain being re-deposited on the surface.

How to tackle a stain

When treating any stain, treat a ring around the stain and then *work from the outside to the middle*; this prevents it from spreading. It is also important to dab at a stain rather than rub it as rubbing may both spread the stain and damage the surface. Where removing a stain has left an amazingly clean spot on something, launder or have it dry-cleaned immediately. Always *use white absorbent cotton cloth* or cotton-wool as a dabber for any solvent or treatment. A coloured fabric dabber may have its dyes affected by certain solvents and cause you to end up with two stains, rather than one, on the original surface.

Professional cleaning is a must if a difficult stain has fallen on to an expensive garment or piece of soft furnishing. Although it's expensive it will certainly pay off in terms of saving the item from permanent marking. Professional dry-cleaners have a battery of cleaning solvents not available on the domestic market and should be able to deal with the most obstinate stains. It is best not to attempt home treatment first as this can complicate and sometimes spoil their work. Be sure to tell them exactly what has been spilled and also to confess if you have had a go at removing it yourself, saying what you used. It is often a help for professional cleaners if you mark round the edge of the stain with tacking stitches—though obviously not on a fabric such as silk where the stitch marks would show.

Stains defined

For home removal purposes, stains can be divided into three groups as follows:

Absorbed stains These are spilled liquids, *eg* tea, coffee, milk or beer, which have been absorbed into a surface. Provided they are treated when they occur, it is usually possible simply to rinse them out of washable fabrics, using lukewarm suds and gently squeezing and rubbing the stained section, fabric to fabric. It is important not to use hot water, which could set the stain. Where you cannot wash an article immediately, leave it soaking in cold water until you can. *Don't* soak wool, silk or any fabric with a flame-resistant finish.

After rubbing the stain in suds, laundering at the temperature recommended for the fabric is usually sufficient to clear any remaining traces. At any rate try this before attacking the traces of stain with a commercial stain remover or a bleach. Immediate use of clear lukewarm water is also the safest way of treating absorbed stains on fabrics which are normally dry-cleaned, provided the fabric is not the type which watermarks. Sponge the stain gently, then blot well with a clean white cloth or unpatterned kitchen paper towel.

Built-up stains These are made by thicker preparations such as grease, nail varnish and paint. They leave a surface deposit but do not generally penetrate far into a surface. The more quickly you can treat them, the less likely they are to set and perhaps cause damage to the surface below. Use paper tissues, towels or a suitable tool such as a metal ruler or back of a knife blade to remove as much of the deposit as possible. Treat any remaining stain according to what caused it (*see* PART 2). Follow treatment by laundering or sponging where necessary.

Compound stains These are caused by substances such as blood which produce a combination of the two types of stain already mentioned, *ie* they penetrate a surface and leave some residue on top. First the deposit should be treated as in built-up stains, then the penetration should be attended to as in absorbed stains. Final laundering or sponging will almost certainly be needed to clear any remaining traces.

OTHER TYPES OF STAIN

Dried and set stains Start with a mild method of removal and, if this fails, move on to something stronger. Part 2 gives details of what to use on what mark. Keep a note of what has been used in what order, in case you have finally to resort to the services of a dry-cleaner.

Mystery stains on fabrics Be very careful with unidentified stains. On washables, soak where possible and then launder. With non-washables, sponge the stained area with clear lukewarm water. after testing on an inconspicuous section if you think the fabric might watermark. Treat obvious grease marks with a grease solvent. Stains that persist can, on washables, be treated with diluted hydrogen peroxide and, on non-washables, with diluted ammonia. Watch carefully to check that colour is not affected by this. If it is or if the stains persist despite treatment, seek professional help.

Stain removal on upholstery Don't over-wet upholstered furniture. It helps to blot up with an old towel as you go along to avoid this. Be particularly careful not to over-wet acrylic velvet, *eg* Dralon, which is woven on to a cotton or cotton/synthetic mixture backing which could shrink and distort the surface.

Water-borne stains can often be removed from Dralon velvet and from non-removable flat-weave Dralon covers by immediate and thorough blotting followed, where necessary, by sprinkling the stain with a weak, warm solution of enzyme detergent (15 ml detergent per litre water) and lightly wiping the way of the pile with a clean sponge. Velvets other than acrylic, and any brocatelles, should be handled professionally. Some dry-cleaners are prepared to come and treat upholstery in your home which, although an expensive service, could work out cheaper than taking your three-piece suite to them.

Stain removal on carpets A squirt from a soda syphon will flush out spilled liquids if used immediately the spill occurs. Remember to keep the syphon always full. Dirty marks and water-soluble stains can be removed usually with carpet shampoo, used according to the manufacturer's instructions. Treat the stain itself with the carpet shampoo then shampoo the whole carpet to avoid a patch showing. Any stain which persists should be treated according to type (*see* PART 2) or professional help must be called in.

When shampooing the stain, mop with an old towel as you go to avoid over-wetting. Where a carpet can be raised, treat the back as well, but take great care with solvents on rubber-latexed or foam-backed carpets.

Following treatment, smooth the carpet pile in the direction in which it lies and allow it to dry naturally (don't apply artificial heat which can damage it) before replacing the furniture.

For water-based stains when you've run out of carpet shampoo, use a solution of 5 ml detergent and 5 ml white vinegar to 1 litre of warm water.

The stain remover's kit

While a stain removal kit, permanently at the ready in your home, can save a lot of money, time and temper, it is important to bear in mind that the majority of items in it are **poisonous**. It should therefore be kept out of the reach of children, preferably locked away. Be sure that all the items in it are labelled clearly. Do not decant anything into another container such as a squash bottle. Most stain removers are used only in small quantities at a time so there is no need to indulge in bulk buying of any item. Little and often would be a more sensible solution.

As we have stressed in the warning note at the beginning of the book, certain solvents which are virtually indispensable in stain removal are **flammable**, while some give off toxic vapours. If possible always open a window in the room where you are using them, or at any rate leave the door open. Wear rubber gloves to avoid any damage to your hands and **never, ever smoke or use solvents in a room where an open fire or radiant heater is burning. Turn off any pilot lights.**

Here is a list of the most useful items to have handy. You may in fact keep a number of them for purposes other than stain removal. It would nonetheless be sensible to invest in a small, additional container of each to keep in your stain removal box. Otherwise you may be sure that the day you need nail varnish remover to get out clear adhesive from a child's cotton shirt will be the day before you planned to buy a new bottle for your dressing table.

Ammonia Household ammonia will remove certain stains and is also good for neutralizing acid marks. It should be used diluted in at least 3 parts of water, always in a well-ventilated room as it gives off unpleasant fumes. Ammonia can cause certain types of dye to bleed so should be tested carefully on coloured fabrics. *Avoid contact with skin, eyes and clothing.*

Enzyme (biological) wash powder This type of detergent is much better than the ordinary kind on protein stains such as blood, egg yolk, milk, gravy and perspiration, where a pre-wash soaking is useful. You should always follow any instructions on length of soak and temperature of water provided by the manufacturer. Make sure the powder is thoroughly dissolved before immersing the article. Enzyme detergent should not be used on protein fibres such as wool or silk, nor on non-colourfast, flame-resistant or rubberized fabrics. It should not be used to soak any item with metal fastenings. When soaking colourfast articles make sure the whole article is immersed in case there is a slight colour change.

Glycerine This is useful for lubricating and softening staining substances on any fabric and colour. A soft stain is always easier to remove by the appropriate method than one that has set hard. Use glycerine diluted in equal parts with warm water. Rub it into the fabric and leave for one hour. Remove by rinsing or sponging with lukewarm water.

Grease solvents Proprietary grease solvents—hereafter called stain removers—remove grease and oil marks and some will also cope with other stains. Check and follow the manufacturer's instructions exactly. Stain removers may be liquid, aerosol or paste. Good ones include Boots Dry Cleaner, Beaucaire, Thawpit and Dabitoff liquids, Goddard's Dry Clean and K2r aerosol and K2r paste (the last two can also be used on wallpaper and stone). All should be used in a well-ventilated room. *Avoid smoking* and excessive inhalation of the vapour. Also avoid excessive contact with the skin or with plastic objects and surfaces.

Hydrogen peroxide This is available from chemists. A mild slow-acting, oxidizing bleach. Buy it in 20 vol strength and use it diluted with 1 part to 6 parts of cold water. It should not be used on nylon or flame-resistant fabrics, but most other fabrics, including silk, can be soaked in the solution for up to 30 minutes, though you should bear in mind that it will have a slow, over-all bleaching action on coloured fabrics. (White articles can be soaked overnight if necessary). To speed the stain removal process on coloureds you can therefore add 2·5 ml ammonia to each litre of hydrogen peroxide and water solution but never add ammonia when the fabric is or contains wool.

Laundry or domestic borax This is a mild alkali which works on acid stains.

Borax is usually used in a solution of 15 ml to 500 ml warm water for sponging or for soaking washable fabrics (10—15 minutes should do the trick). Note that soaking coloured fabrics for any longer could result in slight, over-all bleaching. On white fabrics, sprinkle laundry borax directly on to the dampened stain.

Stretch the fabric over a basin and pour hot water through the stain until it disappears. The big advantage of laundry borax is that it can be used safely on most fabrics.

Methylated spirit An excellent stain-removing solvent, though note that it is *highly flammable and poisonous.* Use it neat, dabbed on to the stain, but check first that colour will not be affected. Methylated spirit should never be used on acetate or triacetate fabrics or on French-polished surfaces where it will dissolve the polish.

White vinegar or dilute acetic acid Both are useful on certain stains and both should be thoroughly rinsed out of fabrics. Never use them on acetate or triacetate fabrics. Take care not to get acetic acid on your skin. Acetic acid can cause dye bleeding so test carefully.

Other solvents Other useful solvents to keep in your kit—nearly all *flammable and dangerous to inhale*—are amyl acetate, white spirit or turpentine substitute, liquid lighter fuel, non-oily nail varnish remover (don't use on acetate or triacetate fabrics), cellulose thinners.

Pre-wash aerosols These are available for use on heavily soiled and stained areas on washable colourfast fabrics; two examples are Frend and Shout. They break down most types of staining matter and loosen ingrained grime so that the residue can then be washed out by the normal laundering process. This eliminates the need for pre-soaking, hard rubbing or scrubbing and boiling.

These sprays should be used on the dry fabric, immediately before laundering. They work best on grease-based soiling and fresh stains; stubborn marks may require two or three treatments. They are not effective on dye staining, paint, permanent ink, rust and blood, although they sometimes effect a slight improvement on old blood stains.

Proprietary kits It is possible to buy kits designed to cope with most household stains. They usually contain a number of small bottles of different chemicals which you use individually or mix together according to the stain. Good ones include the Service-Master First Aid Kit for carpets, rugs and furniture and Holloway's Carpet Care Spot Removing Kit. Other specialized kits are referred to in Part 2 under the particular stain which they remove. For information on where to obtain kits and products that are not readily available in the shops *see* ADDRESSES.

13

2

A-Z of Stain Removal

Adhesives

Scrape off the deposit then treat as follows according to type.

GENERAL NOTE ON ADHESIVES

A number of manufacturers are aware of the problems caused by staining and have formulated their own solvents. These are not normally sold in shops but have to be obtained direct from the manufacturers. You may feel that for the odd gluing job it is not worth obtaining a special solvent but if you are embarking on major DIY work involving adhesives or if your children are keen on making models, it would be sensible to invest in a supply of the appropriate solvent. For details of where to obtain solvents *see* ADDRESSES.

Clear adhesive *eg* Bostik No. 1

on carpets Dab any stain lightly with a pad and non-oily nail varnish remover. If you're not sure what the pile is made of, use amyl acetate but check first for dye bleeding. (*See* page 13.)

on clothes and upholstery Hold an absorbent pad on the right side. From the wrong side dab with a pad and non-oily nail varnish remover. On acetate and triacetate use amyl acetate but check first for dye bleeding.

Contact adhesive *eg* Evo-Stik

on carpets Dab with a pad and non-oily nail varnish remover. If you're not sure what the pile is made of, use lighter fuel or amyl acetate but check first for dye bleeding. (*See* page 13.)

on clothes and upholstery Hold an absorbent pad on the right side. From the wrong side dab with a pad and non-oily nail varnish remover; on acetate and triacetate, use lighter fuel or amyl acetate and check first for dye bleeding.

Epoxy resin *eg* Araldite

on carpets Dab with cellulose thinners. On a synthetic pile carpet or a synthetic fibre mixture use lighter fuel. Dried stains will be impossible to remove but trimming the pile with sharp scissors will often remove a light surface deposit.

on clothes and upholstery Hold a pad over the deposit. Dab from the wrong side with cellulose thinners. On synthetic fibres use lighter fuel. Stains that have dried will be impossible to remove.

Check first with safety rules on page 5

Sticky label backing and adhesive tape

on china, glass and vitreous enamel First soak or rub with a damp cloth. If this fails, rub with white spirit, methylated spirit or cellulose thinners. Do a test area first. Following treatment, wipe surface with a damp cloth.

Latex adhesive *eg* Copydex

on carpets Scrape off surface deposit with the back of a knife blade. The makers of Copydex produce a special solvent which will remove the stain (*see* ADDRESSES).

on clothes and upholstery While still wet, this can be removed with a damp cloth. Once dry, scrape off the deposit and dab the remaining stain with either the manufacturer's solvent or a liquid stain remover. The paint brush cleaner Polyclens Plus will also clear the stain. Do not use paint strippers as they usually contain chemicals which may damage fabrics.

on hard surfaces Gentle rubbing with a clean fingertip will usually roll off latex adhesive, unless it has been allowed to set for some time.

Model-making cement *eg* Humbrol Polystyrene Cement

on carpets, clothing and upholstery Wipe off as much as possible, taking care not to spread the adhesive. Dab the remainder with a pad well moistened with liquid stain remover. Once dried, the cement is extremely difficult to remove but some manufacturers produce a solvent for this (*see* ADDRESSES).

Alcohol *see* BEER; GIN AND OTHER SPIRITS; WINE.

on wood *see* PART 3, FURNITURE, REMOVING MARKS.

Animal stains

blood see BLOOD.

excreta/sick on carpets Remove deposit with absorbent paper or a spoon. Flush the area with a squirt from a soda syphon or sponge with clear, warm water. Blot dry. Use a proprietary pet stain remover to clear and deodorize the area, *eg* Shirley's Savvy or Shaws Pet Stain Remover. If you have a pet stain remover already in the house, use it initially, according to the manufacturer's instructions. Finally shampoo the carpet if necessary. Blot well. (Note that dried matter can sometimes be softened for easier removal by using a pet stain remover).

urine/sick on bedcovers, cushions and upholstery Remove any deposit with absorbent paper, taking care not to spread the mark. Blot dry. If it is not possible to remove the item, try to isolate the affected area by gathering up the fabric and tying white tape or string tightly round it. Rinse under cold running water if possible, or use a pet stain remover, *eg* Shirley's Savvy. Launder or sponge and allow to dry naturally.

urine on carpet Blot up the excess and flush the area with a squirt from a soda syphon or sponge with warm water. Shampoo the carpet. Alternatively use a pet stain remover, *eg* Shirley's Savvy or Shaws Pet Stain Remover, as directed.

Artists' paints

acrylic paint on clothing If still wet, blot off excess paint with absorbent paper and wash out with soap and water. If a stain has dried, place an absorbent pad under it, if possible, and dab the stain with cotton-wool moistened with a liquid stain remover, *eg* Beaucaire, or methylated spirit or use Win-sol Paint Remover and Solvent (*see* ADDRESSES). It is particularly important to do a test area on synthetics. Note that it may not be possible to remove all the colour where a stain has dried completely.

oil paint on clothing Hold an absorbent pad under the stain. Dab the right side with white spirit. Sponge or launder. Where the paint has hardened, use a liquid stain remover such as Beaucaire or

Check first with safety rules on page 5

Win-sol Paint Remover and Solvent (*see* ADDRESSES). It is particularly important to do a test area on synthetics.

poster, powder and water-colour paint on clothes Sponge well with cold water. If necessary leave to soak in cold water. Launder to remove any remaining traces.

Bath stains

(For marks on vitreous or porcelain enamelled baths, *see* below; on plastic baths *see* PART 3, BATHS)

blue/green drip stains Use a proprietary vitreous enamel cleaner recommended by the Vitreous Enamel Development Council for 'bath' or 'general' use (*see* ADDRESSES). On no account use vinegar or any other acid for this purpose as it can damage the glaze.

hard water marks White deposits around taps and waste outlet can be removed as above. Rinse well. Stubborn marks may need a second treatment or a branded sanitary ware cleaner such as RB70.

neglected stains These can usually be removed with a specially formulated sanitary ware cleaner, *eg* RB70. Follow the manufacturer's directions carefully or you may damage the surface of the bath. Train your household to rinse the bath after use to ensure that neglected stains do not occur in future.

rust marks If treatment as for drip stains does not remove rust marks, use a proprietary cleaner with rust-removing properties, *eg* Jenolite Bath Stain Remover, Magica Rust Remover (*see* ADDRESSES). Follow the manufacturer's directions carefully and neutralize with the recommended solvent (usually water).

tide marks Where these do not respond to the treatment given for drip stains, rub with a cloth moistened in white spirit. Wash off immediately with a solution of washing-up liquid and rinse thoroughly. Avoid repetition by encouraging users to clean the bath after each use.

Beer

on carpets Flush fresh stains with a squirt from a soda syphon or sponge with clear warm water. Blot well. Treat any remaining stain or dried marks with a solution of carpet shampoo, *eg* 1001 Dri-Foam, or use a proprietary spotting kit, *eg* Holloway's Carpet Care Spot Removing Kit (*see* ADDRESSES). Gentle sponging with methylated spirit may reduce old stains.

on table linen and washable fabrics Soak fresh stains in luke-warm water or rinse through. Launder as usual. For dried stains on white cottons and linen, launder first then bleach out any remaining stain with a hydrogen peroxide solution (1 part 20 vol hydrogen peroxide to 6 parts cold water). On coloured fabrics (not acetate or triacetate) sponge with a white vinegar solution (30 ml vinegar to 500 ml water). On acetate and triacetate, sponge with a laundry borax solution (15 ml borax to 500 ml warm water). Launder.

on upholstery and non-washable fabrics Blot well and wipe with a cloth wrung out in clear, lukewarm water. Dried stains on non-acetate/triacetate fabrics should be sponged carefully with a white vinegar solution (1 part white vinegar to 5 parts water) and then with clear water. Blot well. Alternatively, and for acetate or tri-acetate fabrics, sponge with clear water, allow to dry naturally, and treat with a proprietary aerosol cleaner such as K2r Stain Remover Spray or Goddard's Dry Clean. On upholstery, a spotting kit (*see* BEER ON CARPETS) can be used.

Beetroot juice

on table linen Rinse immediately in cold water. Use laundry borax

Check first with safety rules on page 5

in solution (15 ml borax to 500 ml warm water) for soaking coloureds. For whites, sprinkle borax in powder form on the dampened stain, then stretch over a basin and pour boiling water through. Soaking and laundering in an enzyme detergent solution is also effective. Dried stains on white fabrics should respond to the use of Dygon Colour and Stain Remover.

Bird droppings

on carpets Wipe or brush up the surface deposit and sponge with warm water. If necessary sponge with a laundry borax solution (15 ml borax to 500 ml warm water). Rinse and blot dry.

on non-washable fabrics and upholstery Wipe or brush up the deposit. Use repeated applications of an aerosol stain remover, *eg* Goddard's Dry Clean, until clear.

on washing on the line Further laundering should remove most stains although it may be necessary to use careful hydrogen peroxide bleaching (1 part 20 vol peroxide to 6 parts cold water) for white and colourfast fabrics (other than nylon) if the bird has been eating berries. A dilute solution of a proprietary bleach, *eg* Brobat, Domestos, Parazone, can be used on white cottons and linens but not on crease-resistant, drip-dry, embossed or piqué fabrics.

Blackberry *see* FRUIT JUICE.

Black-currant *see* FRUIT JUICE.

Blood

on bed sheets and washable fabrics Fresh bloodstains should be sponged immediately with cold salt water, then soaked in a warm enzyme detergent solution according to the maker's directions. Launder in warm suds. Dried stains which do not respond to an enzyme soak may need further soaking in a hydrogen peroxide solution (1 part 20 vol hydrogen peroxide to 6 parts cold water) with added ammonia (2·5 ml ammonia to every 1 litre solution). Don't use hydrogen peroxide on nylon. Rinse well.

on carpets Flush out fresh stains with a squirt from a soda syphon, or sponge well with cold water. Blot dry. If necessary, shampoo area. Alternatively use a proprietary carpet spot removal treatment (*see* ADDRESSES). It may not be possible to clear dried stains.

on mattresses Tip the mattress on to its side and, holding a towel beneath the stained area to avoid spreading the mark, sponge with cold salt water, then clear cold water. The lather from an up-holstery shampoo is usually effective on fresh marks and may also clear dried stains. Treating mattress stains is done more easily by two people—one to hold and one to dab. Mattress covers may ring mark but this is preferable to an untreated stain.

on non-washable fabrics and upholstery Wipe or brush lightly to remove any surface deposit. Sponge with cold water to which you have added a few drops of ammonia (2·5 ml to every 1 litre). Rinse with clear water and blot well. Alternatively use an up-holstery spotting kit (*see* ADDRESSES).

Bottled sauces *see* KETCHUP AND BOTTLED SAUCES.

Brandy *see* GIN AND OTHER SPIRITS.

Bruise marks
on wood *see* PART 3, FURNITURE, REMOVING MARKS.

Burns
on wood *see* PART 3, FURNITURE, REMOVING MARKS.

Butter *see* FATS, GREASE AND OILS.

Candle wax
on carpets Scrape off as much as possible of the deposit with the bowl of a spoon. To melt the remainder, place a sheet of blotting paper or brown paper over it and gently apply the toe of a warm iron to the mark. Do not let the iron touch the pile, which would pro-bably scorch or melt, and keep moving the paper around until all the wax is absorbed. Clear remaining wax with a stain remover, *eg* Goddard's Dry Clean. Remove any remaining colour by dabbing with methylated spirit.

on polished wood surfaces Hold a plastic bag of ice cubes over the wax to harden it thoroughly. Chip at it carefully with a fingernail or plastic spatula. When all deposit is gone, rub with a duster to remove any film. Polish with your usual polish. Where heat mark-ing has occurred, rub hard along the grain with a cloth dipped in metal polish, *eg* Brasso. Hold it over just one finger so that you do not cover an area larger than the mark.

on table linen and washable fabrics Remove surface deposit with a fingernail, taking care not to snag the fabric. Place clean blotting paper both sides of the stain and melt out any remaining wax with a warm iron. Keep moving the paper around for maximum absorption. Apply a stain remover, *eg* Boots Dry Cleaner, to clear remaining traces of wax. Launder to clear any remaining colour left by a coloured candle.

on upholstery fabrics On closely woven fabrics melt out the wax with a moderately hot iron over clean blotting paper. Remove any remaining colour mark by dabbing with methylated spirit (not on acetate or triacetate). On loosely woven fabrics do not attempt to pull off any wax or you may pull threads. Melt it out with an iron and blotting paper. Remove colour traces with methylated spirit. On pile fabrics it is often possible to remove the deposit by rubbing lightly with a cloth. Otherwise use the iron and blotting paper treatment with blotting paper on the pile side and the iron applied to the back. Where this is not possible hold the iron over the blotting paper but without depressing the pile. Clear any traces of wax with an aerosol stain remover, *eg* Goddard's Dry Clean.

on vinyl wall coverings Wait until the wax hardens then lift it off carefully, dabbing gently with methylated spirit to remove any dye left. A liquid householder cleaner, *eg* Handy Andy, should remove any slight stain remaining.

on wallpaper Do not attempt to lift the wax or scrape the paper which will tear away, leaving holes. Use a warm iron over a sheet of blotting paper to melt and absorb the wax. Keep moving the blotting paper around to expose clear surfaces. If a stain remains use an aerosol stain remover, *eg* K2r. Sometimes it may not be possible to remove all traces.

Car and cycle oil

on concrete drives and garage floors Use Holts Garage Floor and Drive Cleaner (*see* ADDRESSES) or Polyclens Plus paint brush cleaner. Neither product is suitable for asphalt surfaces.

Carbon paper

on fabrics Dab the mark lightly with a pad of cotton-wool moistened with methylated spirit. Alternatively, and on acetate and triacetate, use K2r Stain Remover.

Chewing gum

on carpets Use Holloway Chewing Gum Remover (*see* ADDRESSES). This is an aerosol which freezes the deposit so that it can be broken up and brushed clear. Follow the maker's instructions, test an area first, then apply with care as it reaches a low temperature in use and could burn the skin.

on jerseys, worsted trousers, nylon playsuits Place the article in the refrigerator or hold a plastic bag of ice cubes over the deposit to harden it so that it can be cracked and picked off. Any remaining deposit can be removed by a liquid stain remover such as Thawpit (though not on proofed articles) or Swarfega Hand Cleanser rubbed in gently but persistently until the gum dissolves. Launder where possible or sponge the treated area with warm water. Holloway Chewing Gum Remover (*see* opposite) can be tried on difficult deposits following a successful test.

on upholstery Use Holloway Chewing Gum Remover (*see* opposite). Brush up the deposit by hand; the bits could gum up a vacuum cleaner.

Chocolate
on bed linen and washable fabrics Scrape off any deposit with the

Check first with safety rules on page 5

back of a knife blade. Soak, then launder at the temperature recommended for the fabric, using an enzyme detergent if suitable. If stain remains, sprinkle the wet mark with laundry borax powder, stretch the fabric over a basin and pour hot water through. Rinse. Alternatively, use a stain remover such as Beaucaire or Liquid Dabitoff.

on carpets Scrape off as much as possible with a blunt knife. Treat the stained area with carpet shampoo. Treat any remaining stain with a liquid stain remover, *eg* Beaucaire.

on non-washable fabrics Scrape off any deposit with the back of a knife blade. Use a proprietary stain remover such as Liquid Dabitoff or Beaucaire.

Chutney *see* JAM.

Cocoa

on carpets Spoon and blot up as much as possible. Flush out the stain with a squirt from a soda syphon or sponge with warm water. Blot well. Use a carpet shampoo or a carpet spotting kit (*see* ADDRESSES). When dry, remove any traces with a liquid stain remover, *eg* Beaucaire. Dried stains should be sponged well with a laundry borax solution (15 ml borax to 500 ml warm water). Blot dry and if a mark remains, rub in a mixture of equal parts of glycerine and warm water. Leave for up to an hour then rinse and blot. Repeat the glycerine treatment if necessary.

on non-washable fabrics and upholstery Sponge with a laundry borax solution (15 ml borax to 500 ml warm water) then with clear water. Blot dry. Clear any traces when dry by applying a stain remover, *eg* K2r. Alternatively use an upholstery spotting kit (*see* ADDRESSES).

on table linen and washable fabrics Rinse thoroughly in warm water. Soak in a warm enzyme detergent solution if the fabric is suitable. Alternatively soak in a laundry borax solution (15 ml borax to 500 ml warm water) and launder in hand-hot suds. When dry, use a stain remover to remove any traces, *eg* Beaucaire, Liquid Dabitoff. Stubborn marks on white cottons and linens may respond to treatment with Dygon Colour and Stain Remover.

Cod liver oil

on carpets Spoon or blot up the excess and treat with a liquid stain remover, *eg* Polyclens Plus paint brush cleaner. Follow with a dry foam carpet shampoo, *eg* Bissell, and avoid over-wetting. Alternatively, use a carpet spot removal kit (*see* ADDRESSES). With heavy spillage, it may be necessary to treat the stain again after a few days as the oil 'wicks' back.

on non-washable fabrics Dab with a liquid stain remover. On fabrics likely to ring mark use an aerosol stain remover, *eg* Goddard's Dry Clean.

on washable fabrics Before the stain has a chance to dry, launder the garment in a synthetic detergent solution as hot as the fabric will take. Treat dried stains with a liquid stain remover, *eg* Thawpit, then lubricate any remaining marks with a glycerine solution (equal parts glycerine and warm water) and leave for up to an hour before rinsing in clear water followed by laundering. Stubborn marks (not on nylon) may need bleaching out with a hydrogen peroxide solution (1 part 20 vol peroxide to 6 parts cold water).

on woollen garments (babies') Sponge as soon as possible with a warm, fairly concentrated solution of mild detergent such as Dreft. Launder as usual. On dried stains use a liquid stain remover, such as Beaucaire, followed by laundering.

Coffee

on carpets Spoon and blot up as much as possible. Flush out the stain with a squirt from a soda syphon or sponge with warm water and blot dry. This will probably deal with fresh black coffee stains. For remaining marks and white coffee use a carpet shampoo or a carpet spot removal kit (*see* ADDRESSES). When dry, remove any final traces with a stain remover, *eg* Liquid Dabitoff. Dried coffee stains may respond to repeated flushings with a soda syphon. Allow time to dry between each application.

on non-washable fabrics and upholstery Treat as for COCOA on the same surfaces. Coffee stains on acrylic velvet, *eg* Dralon, should be thoroughly blotted with tissue or a cloth. Sprinkle any remaining stain with a warm solution of enzyme washing powder (15 ml powder per 1 litre water) and rub lightly with a sponge in the direction of the pile. This avoids over-wetting. Flat-weave Dralons can be similarly treated. Old stains should be lubricated with a glycerine solution (equal parts glycerine and warm water), left for up to an hour then rinsed with a cloth wrung out in warm water. Blot well.

on table linen and washable fabrics Treat as for COCOA on the same surfaces.

Cosmetics *see* FOUNDATION CREAM; LIPSTICK; LOTIONS.

Crayon

on vinyl wallcoverings and bedheads A wipe with a damp cloth may be sufficient. If not, use a household cleaner, *eg* Handy Andy.
on wallpaper There is no treatment for this. Tear, not cut, another piece of wallpaper to cover the area and paste it over. On dense patterns this should give a fairly invisible mend, though it will tend to show on plain papers.

Cream (edible)   *see* FATS. GREASE AND OILS.

Creosote

on non-washable fabrics Professional cleaning is advisable.
on washable fabrics Hold an absorbent pad on the right side and dab liquid lighter fuel or eucalyptus oil on the wrong side to push the stain out. Launder as usual. Old dried creosote stains are difficult to remove but may be softened sufficiently with glycerine solution (equal parts glycerine and warm water) to be washed out.

Curry

on carpets Scrape up any deposit and rub the stain lightly with a cloth wrung out of a solution of laundry borax (15 ml borax to 500 ml warm water). If this fails, rub a little neat glycerine into the carpet pile, leave for about ten minutes, then sponge out with warm water. Blot dry. This is a difficult stain and large marks should be cleaned professionally.
on non-washable fabrics Sponge with a warm laundry borax solution as for carpets; if this does not remove the stain have the item dry-cleaned professionally.
on table cloths and washable fabrics Rinse well in lukewarm water. Rub in glycerine solution (equal parts glycerine and warm water) leave for an hour and rinse again. Soak and launder, using an enzyme detergent if suitable. Stubborn stains may be bleached out of fabrics other than nylon with a hydrogen peroxide solution (1 part 20 vol hydrogen peroxide to 6 parts cold water).

Cycle oil   *see* CAR AND CYCLE OIL.

Dents

on wood *see* PART 3, FURNITURE, REMOVING MARKS.

Drinks *see* BEER; GIN AND OTHER SPIRITS; WINE.

Duplicating inks

Gestetner duplicating ink

on clothes and upholstery Dab marks with a cotton-wool pad moistened with neat washing-up liquid. Sponge or launder where possible. The manufacturers produce a solvent called Klenzine for removing this ink from hands and clothes (*see* ADDRESSES).

Rank Xerox toner powder

(As used in this firm's duplicating machines.)

on washable fabrics and upholstery Brush, blow or vacuum to remove the powder deposit. Any light marking which remains can be washed out using a lukewarm solution of mild synthetic detergent. Hot water will set the stain.

on non-washable fabrics and upholstery Take these articles for professional cleaning; point out that the stain has been caused by a thermoplastic powder, as certain cleaning solvents will bond the powder to man-made fibres.

Dyes

on floors It is essential to wipe up splashes or spills immediately with a dry absorbent cloth. Avoid the use of water. There is no remedy for dried stains.

on non-washable fabrics, upholstery and carpets Carefully sponge with methylated spirit (not acetate or triacetate fibres) to which you have added a few drops of household ammonia. Alternatively and more safely, have the item dry-cleaned professionally.

on washable fabrics Soak white and fast-coloured fabrics in an enzyme detergent solution (not silk, wool, rubberized or flame-resistant fabrics) to clear discolouration caused by dyes. Launder. Alternatively, on white fabrics, use a proprietary dye stripper, *eg* Dygon Colour and Stain Remover. Silk and wool can be sponged with, or soaked for up to 15 minutes, in a hydrogen peroxide solution (1 part 20 vol hydrogen peroxide to 6 parts cold water). Rinse well and launder.

Egg

on carpets Scrape and use a dry cloth to remove as much of the deposit as possible. Treat with a liquid stain remover, *eg* Beaucaire, followed, where necessary, by a carpet shampoo. Alternatively use a carpet spotting kit (*see* ADDRESSES).

on non-washable fabrics and upholstery Scrape off the surface

Check first with safety rules on page 5

deposit. Sponge egg white with cold salt water then clear water
Blot dry. Use K2r Stain Remover if necessary. On egg yolk work
in the lather from a washing-up detergent solution or upholstery
shampoo. Wipe with a damp cloth. When dry, use a stain remover
eg Dabitoff aerosol, if necessary. For whole egg use a stain
remover or upholstery spotting kit (*see* ADDRESSES).

on table linen and washable fabrics Sponge white of egg with
cold salt water. Rinse. If the stain still shows when dry, soak and
launder in an enzyme detergent solution if the fabric is suitable.
Sponge whole egg with cold salt water then· launder, using an
enzyme detergent where suitable. Dried stains can usually be removed by soaking in an enzyme detergent solution (not silk, wool,
rubberized or flame-resistant fabrics), followed by laundering.
Launder yolk of egg using an enzyme detergent if possible. Apply
an aerosol stain remover when dry to clear any traces, *eg* Dabitoff.

Embroidery transfer

on fabrics This can usually be removed by touching lightly with
methylated spirit (not on acetate or triacetate fabrics) applied on a
cotton bud or cotton-wool wrapped round an orange stick. Test
carefully first on the edge of the fabric. Launder if possible. Where
methylated spirit cannot be used, laundering may be sufficient.

Face cream   *see* FOUNDATION CREAM.

Fats, grease and oils

on carpets Blot up or scrape off deposit. Apply a stain remover, *eg* Beaucaire or Boots Dry Cleaner. Take particular care
where there is a foam or rubber-latexed backing. For heavy deposits
use an iron and blotting paper as described in CANDLEWAX ON
CARPETS. When no more grease can be removed, brush or rub in the
lather from a solution of carpet shampoo, *eg* Bissell, or use an
aerosol foam carpet cleaner, *eg* Johnson Glory. Traces of the
deposit may continue to creep up (called 'wicking back' in the
trade) for some time and you may need to repeat the application.
on leather shoes The maker's preparation of shoe leather, together
with regular cleaning, usually gives a protective surface from which
grease or cooking oil can be wiped without trace—if done quickly.
Some fancy leathers may stain and the use of a rubber adhesive,
as described below for upholstery and handbags, should deal with
this. Alternatively use Meltonian Mel on stubborn marks and
Meltonian Stain Remover on light ones. Clean both shoes completely to disguise any light patches.

on leather upholstery and handbags Cover the stain with a thin layer of bicycle puncture repair adhesive. A test area is essential since most adhesives contain colouring matter which could stain lighter shades. Leave for 24 hours then roll off carefully—it should have absorbed the grease. Treat the article with a good quality hide food, *eg* Leafood, Cee Bee Hide Food.

on non-washable fabrics and upholstery Spread French chalk, talcum powder or powdered starch over a small mark. Replace when it becomes impregnated with oil. Leave for several hours then brush clear. Alternatively, use a proprietary stain remover such as Beaucaire or Boots Dry Cleaner. Take care with foam backings. Grease on flat-woven and velvet-pile Dralon should be treated with Thawpit or Liquid Dabitoff. For larger areas (though not on Dralon or other pile fabrics) press with a warm iron over clean blotting paper to absorb the deposit and finally apply a stain remover, *eg* Beaucaire.

on suède coats Manufacturers of suède coats usually supply a cleaning pad or brush which will remove light stains. Failing this, use a suède cleaning cloth, *eg* Swade Groom, or a cleaning block such as Swade Aid. It is inadvisable to use a liquid cleaner as different types of grease and oil require different treatments and the use of chemicals can affect the dye irrevocably. Large, obvious stains require professional treatment.

on suède shoes Blot the stain with a tissue. Light stains should respond to a block suède cleaner such as Swade Aid. For heavier marking, and after a test on the instep, lightly wipe the stain with a cloth over a pad of cotton-wool which has been moistened with lighter fuel or Meltonian Mel. With the latter it is best to treat the whole shoe to avoid a patchy appearance.

on table linen Blot or scrape off any deposit. Cotton and linen can be laundered at sufficiently high temperatures to remove any marks. Other fabrics should be treated with a stain remover, *eg* Beaucaire, before laundering.

on ties *see* PART 3, TIES.

on wallpaper Use a warm iron over clean blotting paper to draw out as much grease as possible. K2r Stain Remover, in either aerosol or paste form, can be used to clear remaining marks.

For hessian wallcovering use an aerosol stain remover, *eg* K2r Stain Remover, very sparingly and check first for dye change as fairly weak colours are used in hessians.

on washable fabrics Scrape off any deposit. Fabrics that can be laundered in hot water should come clean after this. On other fabrics use a stain remover first, *eg* Beaucaire. Heavy deposits, including car and cycle oil, should be rubbed with Polyclens Plus paint brush cleaner or Swarfega Hand Cleanser before laundering. Delicate fabrics and wool should be dabbed with eucalyptus oil then laundered or sponged.

Fish oil *see* FATS, GREASE AND OILS.

Flower stains

on clothes Laundering will usually remove these. Otherwise rub the marks with methylated spirit (not on acetate or triacetate fabrics) then sponge with warm water.

in vases and bowls Fill them with water to which you have added a few drops of household bleach, *eg* Domestos, or denture cleaner, *eg* Steradent. Allow to soak for half an hour then rinse. Alternatively use a stain remover such as Chempro T.

Fly specks

on fabric lampshades Try the careful use of an aerosol stain remover, *eg* K2r or Goddard's Dry Clean. If this fails, make up a warm solution of a heavy duty detergent, *eg* Persil, and brush over the stains from both sides using a soft brush (an old, soft toothbrush would be good). Rinse the area in the same way with clear water. Blot and allow to dry naturally away from direct heat in order to prevent ring marking or splitting. Do not wet the trimming.

on upholstery fabrics Dab with a stain remover, *eg* Thawpit, or methylated spirit (not on acetate or triacetate materials). Test first. Alternatively try an aerosol stain remover, *eg* Goddard's Dry Clean.

on vellum and plastic lampshades Wipe with a damp cloth wrung out in soapy water. Wipe with clear water and allow to dry.

Foundation cream

on upholstery and non-washable fabrics Wipe up any wet deposit carefully. Brush a dried stain with a soft brush to clear any powder. Apply a stain remover using an aerosol, *eg* K2r, for fabrics which might ring mark with liquids. Alternatively, talcum powder or French chalk can be rubbed into light-coloured fabrics; after 2 hours shake and brush lightly with a soft-bristled brush. An upholstery spotting kit (*see* ADDRESSES) may also be used.

on washable fabrics Wipe a fresh stain to clear the surface deposit and, where possible, soak for 5 minutes in a weak ammonia solution (5 ml ammonia to 500 ml warm water). Rinse well. Launder at the highest temperature suited to the fabric. Dried stains should be brushed to remove the powder content, softened by lubricating with a glycerine solution (equal parts glycerine and warm water) left on up to an hour, before laundering.

Fruit juice

on carpets Scoop up and absorb as much as possible with paper towels. Shampoo the area and, when dry, remove any remaining traces by dabbing with a cloth moistened in methylated spirit.

on table linen Rinse under a cold tap then stretch the stained part of the fabric over a basin and pour hot water through it. Lubricate any remaining stain with a glycerine solution (equal parts glycerine and warm water), leave for an hour and launder as usual. Dried stains may need to be covered with laundry borax powder before hot water is poured through. Alternatively soak the stained area in an enzyme detergent solution before laundering. On white fabrics, Dygon Colour and Stain Remover will remove marks.

on upholstery and non-washable fabrics Sponge with cold water and blot dry. Use an upholstery stain removal kit (*see* ADDRESSES) or a Spotkleen impregnated cleaning cloth.

on washable fabrics Rinse under a cold tap. When clear water rinsing fails, stains on white silk, nylon and wool may respond to the use of Dygon Colour and Stain Remover. For other articles, soak and launder with enzyme detergent if the fabric is suitable.

Check first with safety rules on page 5

Dried stains should be lubricated with glycerine solution (equal
parts glycerine and warm water) and left up to an hour before treating as suggested. Very stubborn stains on fabrics other than nylon
may respond to careful bleaching with a hydrogen peroxide solution (1 part 20 vol peroxide to 6 parts cold water). White fabrics
can be soaked in a proprietary nappy soak, *eg* Napisan, following
the manufacturer's instructions.

Gin and other spirits

on carpets Blot up excess fluid and flush the mark with a squirt
from a soda syphon or sponge with a cloth lightly wrung out in
warm water. Blot well. If staining remains, apply the lather of a
carpet shampoo, *eg* Bissell, or use a carpet spotting kit (*see*
ADDRESSES). Sponging with methylated spirit may reduce old stains.
on non-washable fabrics and upholstery Sponge with clear lukewarm water then blot dry. If staining remains, apply the lather from
an upholstery shampoo solution or washing-up detergent. Rub
lightly then wipe clear with a cloth wrung out in warm water and
blot dry. Alternatively, use an upholstery spotting kit (*see*
ADDRESSES).

In the case of fabrics which would water mark, these should be
taken for professional cleaning.
on table cloths and washable fabrics Rinse with clear warm water
then launder as usual.
on wood *see* PART 3, FURNITURE, REMOVING MARKS.

Grass stains

on cricket flannels If washable, light staining should come out with
laundering. Heavier marks should first be dabbed with methylated

spirit then rinsed in clear water. Flannels which are normally dry-cleaned should be rubbed with a mixture of equal parts of cream of tartar powder and free-flow salt. Leave for 10 minutes then brush clear. Alternatively use the liquid stain remover Beaucaire or K2r aerosol, repeating applications if necessary or have the flannels dry-cleaned.

on washable clothes Light staining should wash out. With heavier marks, dab with methylated spirit (not on acetate and triacetate materials) then rinse in clear water before laundering.

Gravy

on carpets Scoop up excess and wipe with a dry cloth to remove as much as possible. Treat with a liquid stain remover such as Boots Dry Cleaner followed by a carpet shampoo. Alternatively, use a carpet spotting kit (*see* ADDRESSES). Blot frequently to avoid over-wetting.

on non-washable fabrics Treat with a stain remover, *eg* Beaucaire. Wipe with a cloth wrung out in *warm* water provided the fabric doesn't watermark.

on table linen and washable fabrics Soak in cool water then launder in warm detergent suds. Treat any grease marks remaining when dry with a stain remover, *eg* Liquid Dabitoff. Dried stains should be soaked in an enzyme detergent solution (not silk, wool, rubberized or flame-resistant fabrics) before laundering.

Hair oil

on fabric-upholstered headboards Treat with a stain remover, *eg* Thawpit or Liquid Dabitoff (both specially recommended for Dralons), or Goddard's Dry Clean. Do not over-apply, particularly on padded areas. Avoid marks recurring by treating the headboard with a protective spray, *eg* Scotchgard Fabric Protector.

on wooden headboards Rub with a cloth moistened in white spirit. Buff well with a soft dry cloth.

HAIR OIL ON WALLCOVERINGS

on hessian Treat as for FATS, GREASE AND OILS on hessian wall-coverings.

on painted walls Wipe the stained area gently with a general purpose household cleaner used neat. Dab with a cloth wrung out in clear water.

on wallpaper Treat as for FATS, GREASE AND OILS on wallpaper.

on washable wallpaper Sponge the mark with a warm, well

diluted washing-up liquid solution. Rinse with a cloth wrung out in clear water and pat dry.

on vinyl Wipe gently with a cloth wrung out in a solution of general purpose household cleaner and rinse. Stubborn marks should be rubbed lightly with white spirit.

Hair spray

on mirrors Wipe with a cloth moistened in methylated spirit.

Heat marks

on wood see PART 3, FURNITURE, REMOVING MARKS.

Ice cream

on carpets Scrape up the deposit and wipe with a damp cloth to remove as much of the staining as possible. Apply a carpet shampoo. Alternatively use a carpet spotting kit (*see* ADDRESSES). Any grease marks which remain after the carpet has dried should be treated with a stain remover, *eg* Goddard's Dry Clean or Beaucaire.

on non-washable fabrics and upholstery Wipe off surface deposit. Sponge with lukewarm water. When dry treat any stain with a stain remover, *eg* Goddard's Dry Clean or Beaucaire. Remaining traces can be bleached out carefully with a hydrogen peroxide solution (1 part 20 vol peroxide to 6 parts cold water) if the fabric is suitable (not on nylon).

on washable fabrics Wipe off excess and soak in warm detergent suds. Use an enzyme detergent if the fabric is suitable. Launder in water as hot as the fabric can take. On fabrics that cannot be soaked, such as silk and wool, and also on other fabrics where the stain has dried, sponge with a warm laundry borax solution (15 ml borax to 500 ml water) before laundering. When dry, treat any grease marks with a stain remover, such as Beaucaire, and bleach out any remaining stain with a hydrogen peroxide solution (1 part 20 vol hydrogen peroxide to 6 parts cold water) if the fabric is suitable (not on nylon).

Ink

on wood see PART 3, FURNITURE, REMOVING MARKS.

Ballpoint ink

on fabrics and upholstery Act quickly or the stain may become impossible to remove. Most types respond to light dabbing with methylated spirit applied on a cotton-wool bud. If a test section proves unsuccessful, contact the pen manufacturer for advice. Launder, if possible, after treatment. Obtain professional treatment for delicate fabrics, jacket linings and intensive staining.

on suède handbags Try rubbing lightly with a fine emery cloth or the suède cleaning block Swade Aid. Failing this seek professional advice. It may not be possible to remove this stain.

on vinyl upholstery, wallcoverings, dolls and handbags Unless treated immediately this stain cannot be removed as the ink quickly merges into the plasticizer and causes permanent marking. Treatment is to scrub at once with a nail brush, using warm water and soap or detergent.

Felt-tip ink

on fabrics and upholstery Small marks should be dabbed with methylated spirit (never use on acetate or triacetate materials). Where possible launder using soap powder or flakes. Alternatively use the aerosol stain remover K2r.

on vinyl bedheads, wallcoverings, dolls and handbags Carefully use a household cleaner, *eg* Handy Andy, or methylated spirit. If these fail use neat washing-up liquid applied on a cloth over one finger. Finish with a car vinyl cleaner, *eg* Holts Brush-Up.

It is worth contacting individual manufacturers for advice about heavy staining from their pens. Professional cleaning is advised for delicate fabrics and extensive staining.

Fountain-pen ink

on carpets Flush with a squirt from a soda syphon then blot with absorbent paper. Remove as much further ink as possible by sponging with warm water, blotting to avoid over-wetting. Apply a small quantity of dry foam carpet shampoo. Repeat as necessary, blotting well between applications. Any small stains remaining on light-coloured carpets can be treated with a solution of sodium hydrosulphite (obtainable in powder form from certain chemists), using 25 ml sodium hydrosulphite to 600 ml water. Do a test first as it has a bleaching action. If satisfactory, apply small amounts, blotting between each. Rinse with warm water. Alternatively use a carpet spotting kit after initial blotting. Old stains usually require professional treatment, though if you know the type of ink spilt, the manufacturer (*see* ADDRESSES) may be able to suggest a process.

on fabrics and upholstery Act quickly to prevent the stain drying. Sponge with, or rub under, cold water until no more ink can be removed. Launder if possible to clear traces. If marks remain after laundering, squeeze lemon juice over them and press the stained area between two pieces of white cotton cloth. Repeat as necessary, then rinse. Treat fresh stains on upholstery with an upholstery spotting kit (*see* ADDRESSES). Where this is not available, sponge gently with warm water and blot well to remove as much as possible. When dry, follow with repeated applications of a stain remover, *eg* K2r, to clear any traces.

Dried stains on white fabrics should respond to Dygon Colour and Stain Remover or a weak solution of household bleach (though not on silk, wool, crease-resistant or drip-dry fabrics). Dried stains on coloureds may be removed by repeated applications of a stain remover, *eg* K2r. Stains on delicate fabrics, expensive articles and upholstery should be treated professionally.

For washable blue Super Quink, Parker recommend that both fresh and dried stains are rinsed in cold water. If necessary, apply cotton-wool pads soaked in hot soap solution (not detergent). Leave the pads for 15 minutes, then replace as necessary.

Iodine

on carpets Using a cotton-wool pad, carefully dab with a solution of photographic hypo (2·5 ml to 250 ml warm water). This is obtainable from chemists stocking photographic materials. As soon as the stain has been cleared, treat the area with a warm carpet shampoo solution. Blot to avoid over-wetting.

on non-washable fabrics and upholstery Professional dry-cleaning is recommended.

on washable fabrics and bedding Immediate laundering in rich soap suds with a few drops of ammonia added usually clears the stain. Soak stubborn and dried stains briefly in a solution of photographic hypo (2·5 ml to 250 ml warm water). This is obtainable from chemists stocking photographic materials. Rinse well and launder in the usual way.

Iron mould (rust marking)

on table linen and handkerchiefs Rub with lemon juice, cover the stain with salt and leave for up to an hour. Rinse and launder. If stains persist use a proprietary rust remover, *eg* Movol, Magica (*see* ADDRESSES), and rinse well with the fabric held horizontally under a cold running tap. For large white articles use Dygon.

Jam, marmalade

on carpets Scoop up and wipe off any surface deposit with a cloth wrung out in warm water. Treat the area with a carpet shampoo. Alternatively use a carpet spotting kit (*see* ADDRESSES). Any fruit colour remaining should respond to dabbing with methylated spirit.

on non-washable fabrics and upholstery Wipe off any surface deposit. Sponge the stain with a cloth moistened in a warm solution of washing-up liquid. If marks persist, rub on a little laundry borax powder, leave for a few minutes, then sponge clear. Alternatively sponge the stain with clear warm water, allow to dry and apply K2r Stain Remover or an upholstery spotting kit (*see* ADDRESSES).

on table linen and washable fabrics Fresh stains can usually be washed out. Old stains should first be soaked in a laundry borax solution (15 ml borax to 500 ml warm water) for half an hour, or in an enzyme detergent solution (where the fabric is suitable), then laundered.

Ketchup and bottled sauces

on carpets Scoop and wipe up excess with a clean damp cloth, being careful not to spread the stain. Dried stains can sometimes be softened by rubbing in a 50 : 50 solution of glycerine and water. Sponge with clean warm water, blotting to avoid over-wetting. Gently rub lather from a whisked-up solution of carpet shampoo on to any remaining stain. Wipe in the direction of the pile with a cloth wrung out in lukewarm water. When dry, repeated applications of an aerosol stain remover, *eg* K2r, should clear any traces.

on upholstery and non-washable fabrics Scrape carefully with the back of a knife to remove excess. Wipe lightly with a clean damp cloth. Apply an aerosol stain remover, *eg* K2r, when the fabric has dried. Professional treatment is advised for tomato-based sauces and delicate fabrics.

on washable fabrics Gather up the stained area and rinse under a cold tap. Sponge in a warm solution of Stergene then rinse well. If staining remains, soak (not wool, silk, *etc*) in a biological washing powder solution and launder using the same detergent.

Lipstick

on carpets Scrape carefully with a blunt knife to remove any surface deposit, then treat with a stain remover such as Polyclens Plus paint brush cleaner or a carpet spot removal kit (*see* ADDRESSES). Clear indelible lipstick colour by careful application of methylated spirit.

Check first with safety rules on page 5

... and thank you for providing such a very agreeable lady curate!

on gloss- or emulsion-painted walls and vinyl wallcoverings Rub
the marks lightly with a damp cloth or one wrung out in a warm detergent solution. Stubborn marks may respond to a cream-type
household cleaner such as Jif.

on non-washable fabrics and upholstery Dab gently with
eucalyptus oil or use a liquid stain remover such as Boots Dry
Cleaner.

on table linen, towels and other washable fabrics Most stains
will wash out although some types of lipstick may need an initial
application of a suitable liquid stain remover, *eg* Beaucaire
Indelible lipstick marks should be softened before washing by
rubbing in glycerine solution (equal parts glycerine and warm water)
or eucalyptus oil. Rinse in clear water. Remaining marks on white
fabrics should be bleached out of fabrics other than nylon with a
hydrogen peroxide solution (1 part 20 vol peroxide to 6 parts cold
water).

on wallpaper K2r Stain Remover, in aerosol or paste form, can be
used on this. Stubborn marks and indelible lipstick may need to be
covered by a new piece of wallpaper. If torn rather than cut to shape
it will be less obvious when stuck on the wall.

Lotions
If greasy treat as under FATS, GREASE AND OILS.
If non-greasy treat as under GIN AND OTHER SPIRITS.

Marmalade *see* JAM.

Mascara
on towels, clothes and upholstery Apply an aerosol stain remover such as Goddard's Dry Clean. If a stain still remains, dab with diluted ammonia (1 part ammonia to 3 parts cold water) but test coloureds as ammonia can cause dyes to run. Rinse the area thoroughly. Launder where possible.

Mayonnaise
on non-washable fabrics Remove the residue with a damp cloth, taking care not to spread the stain. Treat the dry fabric with an aerosol stain remover such as K2r. Professional cleaning is advisable for expensive garments.
on table linen and washable fabrics Sponge with warm water (not hot which would set the egg content). Use an enzyme detergent to soak where possible, then launder in rich suds.

Medicines
Sponging with warm water followed by laundering, where possible, should remove most medicines, though methylated spirit may be necessary to take out final colour traces. It is sensible to consult a chemist as to what is in a particular medicine before attempting treatment.

Metal polish
on carpets Spoon and blot up as much as possible. Dab the area with white spirit. Use a stiff carpet brush to clear the powdery deposit when the pile has dried. Shampoo if necessary. Dried stains should be brushed before treatment is applied. The manufacturers of Brasso produce a solvent for its removal (*see* ADDRESSES).
on fabrics Wipe with a tissue to clear as much of the deposit as possible. Apply a stain remover such as Boots Dry Cleaner. Laundering should remove traces from washable fabrics. On non-washable fabrics sponge off as much as possible and brush well when dry. Treat any remaining marks with a stain remover. The

---

Check first with safety rules on page 5

solvent available for Brasso on carpets can also be used on fabrics (*see* ADDRESSES).

Mildew

on leather shoes and cases Sponge the leather with a mild disinfectant solution, *eg* pine (5 ml disinfectant to 500 ml warm water). Alternatively, wipe over with a cotton-wool pad moistened with an antiseptic mouth wash, used neat. Wipe and buff dry with a soft cloth. Follow with an application of a good quality hide food, *eg* Connolly's Cee Bee Hide Food, or shoe polish in the case of shoes.

on non-washable fabrics and upholstery Spray with Mystox solution (*see* ADDRESSES). The smell should disappear after 3 or 4 days. For articles of value it is sensible to consult a museum such as the Victoria and Albert (*see* ADDRESSES).

on plastic shower curtains Sponge with a weak solution of household bleach or antiseptic to clear light marking. Areas heavily stained with this minute fungus-like growth can be swabbed with a mild detergent solution then rinsed with a solution of a proprietary bactericide, *eg* Fungo (*see* ADDRESSES).

on wall surfaces Wash down the wall with a mild detergent solution. Follow by wiping over with a solution of a proprietary bactericide, *eg* Fungo (*see* ADDRESSES).

on washable fabrics Laundering usually removes mildew marking while the growth is still fresh enough to be on the surface. Traces which remain on white fabrics (except nylon) can be treated by bleaching with a hydrogen peroxide solution (1 part 20 vol peroxide to 6 parts cold water). Household bleach can be used on white cottons or linens (though not on crease-resistant, drip-dry, embossed or piqué fabrics). On coloureds, rub the dampened areas with hard soap and dry in the sun. Regular washing will reduce marks.

Milk

on carpets Speedy treatment is vital to stop penetration and dry-ing, otherwise the smell is virtually impossible to eradicate. Use a soda syphon or lukewarm water to flush the area well and blot thoroughly. Next use a carpet shampoo or carpet spot removal kit (*see* ADDRESSES). If a stain remains when the carpet is dry, apply a stain remover, *eg* Beaucaire, but do not allow it to soak on to a rubber-latexed or foam backing. Although it may be pos-sible to remove dried stains yourself, professional cleaning may still be necessary to clear the smell which becomes apparent when-ever the room warms up.

on non-washable fabrics and upholstery Sponge with lukewarm water. If a stain remains when the fabric is dry, use a stain re-mover, *eg* Goddard's Dry Clean, Thawpit (recommended for use on Dralons). Alternatively, use an upholstery spotting kit (*see* ADDRESSES).

on table linen and washable fabrics Rinse well in lukewarm water then launder in warm detergent suds. When dry, treat any remaining mark with a stain remover, *eg* Beaucaire. Dried stains can be soaked before laundering in an enzyme detergent solution, if the fabric is suitable, otherwise, with the exception of nylon, in a hydrogen peroxide solution (1 part 20 vol hydrogen peroxide to 6 parts cold water).

Mud

on carpets Allow the mud to dry completely, then brush off with a stiff-bristled carpet brush and vacuum. Use a carpet shampoo, *eg* Bissell, Johnson Glory, or a carpet spotting kit (*see* ADDRESSES). Any colour traces that remain should be dabbed lightly with methylated spirit.

on non-washable fabrics and upholstery Allow the mud to dry completely then lightly brush off. Sponge remaining marks with a warm, mild detergent solution. Wipe with a cloth wrung out in clear water and blot well. On coats (not waterproof) and heavy clothing, use a stain remover such as Boots Dry Cleaner on marks remaining after the initial brushing.

on washable fabrics Laundering should remove mud staining but use a soft brush on dried deposits and treat heavy marking with a stain remover such as Boots Dry Cleaner before washing as usual.

Mustard
Ready-mixed English mustard

on non-washable fabrics Where a fabric will not ring mark, sponge with a solution of mild synthetic detergent, *eg* Dreft, and remove any remaining colour by sponging with an ammonia solution (5 ml ammonia to 500 ml water). Blot with a towel to avoid over-wetting and finish with clear water. Delicate fabrics and those likely to ring mark should be treated professionally. It is important to tell the cleaner which type of mustard is involved.

on table linen and washable fabrics Wash the stained area in a warm solution of mild synthetic detergent, *eg* Dreft, then remove any remaining stain by sponging with an ammonia solution (5 ml ammonia to 500 ml water). Launder.

Powdered (made-up) mustard

For prepared varieties of American, French and German mustard, follow the same procedure.

on non-washable fabrics Professional dry-cleaning is recommended. Tell the cleaner which type of mustard is involved.

on washable fabrics Laundering should clear the stain. Lubricate dried stains with a glycerine solution (equal parts glycerine and warm water) and leave for up to an hour before laundering.

Nail varnish

on carpets Scoop and carefully wipe up as much of the deposit as possible with paper tissues, trying to avoid spreading the stain. Dab the mark with a pad of cotton-wool moistened with amyl acetate, after testing near the edge of the carpet. A pad with non-oily nail varnish remover can also be used following an initial test. Over-soaking with these solvents could damage carpet backings. Alternatively use a carpet spotting kit (*see* ADDRESSES). Any remaining colour should respond to dabbing with methylated spirit. Finish by applying a foam carpet shampoo, or the lather of a carpet shampoo solution to the treated area.

on fabrics and upholstery Wipe up spills immediately, using absorbent paper or cotton-wool. Where possible, hold a white absorbent pad beneath the stain and dab with amyl acetate (safe on most fabrics but a test area is advised). A pad with non-oily nail varnish remover can also be used, but not on acetates and tri-acetates. Any colouring remaining can usually be cleared by dabbing with methylated spirit but this should never be used on acetate or triacetate. Launder the fabric where possible. Heavy spills on acetate and triacetate need professional cleaning.

Nicotine *see* TOBACCO STAINS.

Oil *see* CAR AND CYCLE OIL; FATS, GREASE AND OILS; HAIR OIL; PARAFFIN OIL.

Orange juice *see* FRUIT JUICE.

Paints

GENERAL NOTE
More recently-developed types of paint, where cleaning the brushes in a washing-up liquid solution is recommended in the in-structions, can usually be removed from most surfaces by launder-ing or sponging immediately (don't wait until you've finished the painting job). It is essential in fact to treat all paint spills speedily as dried paint marks of any kind are very difficult to remove. With all paint spills, first scrape and wipe off as much as possible and then treat according to type. (See also ARTISTS' PAINTS.)

Emulsion and water-based undercoat
Treat wet paint by sponging immediately with cold water, taking care to mop carefully round the edges to avoid spreading the stain. Launder in warm suds where possible. With dried emulsion stains, use methylated spirit to soften the deposit but take care that it does not affect any colour (do not use on acetate or tri-acetate fabrics). Alternatively use Polyclens Plus paint brush cleaner. Follow by laundering or sponging. Delicate fabrics and large areas of dried emulsion on upholstery, carpets or clothing are best treated professionally—avoid home efforts.

Gloss (oil-based) and oil-based undercoat
Dab carefully with white spirit or Polyclens Plus paint brush cleaner after an initial test. Sponge with cold water and repeat the treatment if necessary. Launder where possible; shampoo

Check first with safety rules on page 5

carpets and upholstery. Alternatively use a carpet or upholstery spotting kit (*see* ADDRESSES). Treat dried stains with a paint brush cleaner or, as a last resort, a chemical paint remover. Test first. Bad marks and acetate and viscose fabrics need professional treatment.

Paraffin oil

on carpets Do not smoke as paraffin is highly flammable. Tackle the mark at once as oil which penetrates to the back of a carpet can cause dye seepage and deterioration of foam or rubber-latexed backing. Mop up as much as possible with absorbent paper or rags then use an aerosol stain remover, such as Goddard's Dry Clean or K2r, repeating applications until the mark clears. Large areas of stain should be cleaned professionally.

on non-washable fabrics Treat as FATS, GREASE AND OILS on non-washable fabrics.

on washable fabrics Treat as FATS, GREASE AND OILS on washable fabrics.

Perfume

on non-washable fabrics Lubricate with a glycerine solution (equal parts glycerine and warm water), leave for up to an hour then wipe carefully with a cloth wrung out in warm water, taking care not to over-wet the fabric. Blot dry. Expensive clothes, particularly silk, should be cleaned professionally.

on washable fabrics Rinse immediately. If the stain has dried, lubricate with a glycerine solution (equal parts glycerine and warm water) and leave for up to an hour before laundering as usual.

Perspiration

on non-washable fabrics Dab with a solution of white vinegar (15 ml vinegar to 250 ml warm water) which should help both to clear the stain and deodorize the area. Where dye has been affected, light rubbing with methylated spirit may help. Neither should be used on acetate or triacetate and they could damage some viscose fabrics. Men's suits are often lined with these fabrics and should be cleaned professionally, as should any garments that are heavily stained.

on washable fabrics Sponge fresh stains with a weak solution of ammonia (15 ml ammonia to 500 ml warm water) and rinse immediately. Where colour has been affected sponge with a white vinegar solution (15 ml vinegar to 250 ml warm water) and rinse. Suitable fabrics can be soaked in an enzyme detergent solution.

Alternatively, white fabrics other than nylon can usually be bleached with a hydrogen peroxide solution (1 part 20 vol peroxide to 6 parts cold water). Finally, launder as usual, adding a little vinegar to the rinse water.

Pitch *see* TAR.

Plasticine
on jerseys, worsted trousers, carpets and upholstery Carefully scrape off as much as possible. Hold an absorbent pad under the stain, if possible, and dab it with a liquid stain remover, *eg* Thawpit, Dabitoff, to dissolve the deposit. On small areas, dabbing with liquid lighter fuel may do the trick but this needs care on synthetic fabrics. Avoid dampening the carpet backing. Washable fabrics should then be laundered as usual, non-washables sponged gently with warm water and blotted dry at once.

Rain spots
on calf leather coats, handbags, shoes Before the spots dry, wipe with a clean cloth then allow to dry naturally.
on suède clothes Allow rain spots to dry naturally, then use the manufacturer's special suède cleaning pad, a soft bristled brush or a suède cleaning cloth such as Swade Groom.
on suède shoes Treat as for suède clothes. *See* also PART 3, LEATHER.

Raspberry *see* FRUIT JUICE.

Resins *see* CREOSOTE; SHELLAC.

Ribena *see* FRUIT JUICE.

Rubber
perished from hot-water bottles on sheets, hot-water bottle covers Hold an absorbent pad below the mark and rub with liquid lighter fuel. Launder as usual.

Rum *see* GIN AND OTHER SPIRITS.

Rust marks
on bath see BATH STAINS.
on carpets use a proprietary rust remover, *eg* Magica (*see* ADDRESSES), following the maker's instructions.

Check first with safety rules on page 5

on non-washable fabrics Use a proprietary rust remover, *eg* Magica (*see* ADDRESSES), following the maker's instructions.

on washable fabrics Rub marks with neat lemon juice then rinse. Alternatively use a proprietary rust remover, such as Movol (white fabrics only) or Magica (*see* ADDRESSES). Launder as usual.

Salad dressing *see* FATS, GREASE AND OILS, or MAYONNAISE, according to type.

Salt and water marking
on calf leather boots Re-dampen the mark with a sponge or cloth, then dry off by rubbing with a soft absorbent cloth. Failing this, use Meltonian Stain Remover on the stain and then lightly over the whole boot or shoe to counteract any colour change.

on suède shoes Allow the suède to dry out naturally then use a proprietary stain remover, *eg* Meltonian Stain Remover.

Scent *see* PERFUME.

Scorch marks
on carpets Where scorching is slight it may be possible to trim the tufts with scissors. Otherwise use a stiff-bristled brush to remove any loosened fibres. Then take a wire brush or piece of coarse glass-

paper and make gentle circular movements to hide the area. Some carpet retailers are prepared to re-tuft or patch damaged areas but this is an expensive job to have done.

on non-washable fabrics Use a glycerine solution (equal parts glycerine and warm water) to lubricate light marks, leave up to an hour then sponge with warm water. On heavier marks, sponge with a cloth wrung out in a laundry borax solution (15 ml borax to 500 ml warm water). Rinse and repeat treatment if necessary, taking care not to over-wet.

on washable fabrics Light marks should be rubbed, fabric to fabric, under cold running water, then soaked in a warm laundry borax solution (15 ml borax to 500 ml warm water) until clear. Rinse and launder as usual. Heavy marks cannot usually be removed completely, although those on white fabrics, except nylon, will sometimes respond to careful bleaching with a hydrogen peroxide solution (1 part 20 vol peroxide to 6 parts cold water).

Scratches
on wood see PART 3, FURNITURE, REMOVING MARKS.

Sea water marks *see* SALT AND WATER MARKING.

Shellac
on non-washable fabrics Act quickly before it has a chance to dry and harden. Dab lightly with a cotton-wool pad moistened with methylated spirit (not on acetate or triacetate fabrics). Follow by wiping with a cloth wrung out of a warm synthetic detergent solution. Finish with clear water and blot well. Professional treatment will be necessary for delicate fabrics and dried stains.

on washable fabrics Act immediately, dabbing the stain with methylated spirit (not on acetate or triacetate fabrics). Once the shellac has dried, it may be possible to soften it sufficiently with methylated spirit so that any remaining deposit and colour can be laundered or sponged out with a synthetic detergent solution.

Shoe polish
on carpets Scrape off as much of the deposit as possible. Dab either with a stain remover or white spirit to dissolve any remaining particles. If any stain remains, dab with methylated spirit and finally shampoo the treated area. Alternatively treat the mark with a carpet spotting kit (*see* ADDRESSES) after scraping off the deposit.

Check first with safety rules on page 5

on non-washable fabrics Scrape off as much of the deposit as possible. Treat as for carpets (above) and finish off by sponging with warm water then blotting dry.

on washable fabrics Either use a stain remover, *eg* Polyclens Plus, to remove the mark, or use a few drops of ammonia in the water when laundering. Heavy marking will need treatment with a liquid stain remover such as Polyclens Plus or white spirit before rinsing and laundering.

Smoke and soot

on brickwork Use a soft brush or vacuum cleaner attachment to remove soot, then scrub with a hard scrubbing brush and clear warm water. If soiling does not respond, try wiping down with malt vinegar (this may also remove burn marks), followed by thorough rinsing. Heavy soot staining may need to be treated with a solution of spirits of salts (1 part spirits of salts to 6 parts water), but do not allow it to come into contact with the cement between the bricks. Wash down quickly and thoroughly with plenty of warm water. **Spirits of salts is corrosive,** so wear gloves and goggles and protect clothing; it also gives off extremely strong and **poisonous fumes,** so see that the room is well ventilated and do not lean over the surface while applying the solution.

on carpets Do not brush as this might spread the mark. Vacuum the area or shake the carpet or rug gently, out of doors if possible. Small marks will usually come out with an aerosol stain remover, such as K2r. Large areas of stain are best cleaned professionally, though they may respond to light brushing with the lather of a carpet shampoo solution. On light-coloured carpets, use repeated applications of French chalk or Fuller's Earth. Rub in lightly and vacuum off when the powder has absorbed the soot.

on stonework Follow fireplace manufacturer's cleaning instructions when available. Otherwise scrub with clear water. Use a mild solution of washing-up liquid on light marks and a concentrated solution of domestic bleach on heavy marks. Rinse thoroughly.

Soft drinks *see* FRUIT JUICE.

Soup *see* KETCHUP AND BOTTLED SAUCES.

Spirit *see* GIN AND OTHER SPIRITS.

Sweat *see* PERSPIRATION.

Syrup *see* JAM.

Tar

on carpets Scrape gently to remove the deposit. Very hard marks may be given an initial softening with a glycerine solution (equal parts glycerine and warm water). Leave for up to an hour then rinse with clear water and blot well. Use either a carpet spotting kit (*see* ADDRESSES) or, when dry, a stain remover, *eg* K2r, Beaucaire. Obstinate stains will sometimes respond to dabbing with eucalyptus oil, Polyclens Plus paint brush cleaner or Swarfega Hand Cleanser, lightly rubbed into the pile.

on non-washable fabrics Treat as tar on carpets, above.

on leather shoes After an initial test on the instep, try dabbing with liquid lighter fuel or use Meltonian Mel.

on suède shoes Following a successful test, try a very careful application of liquid stain remover, *eg* Thawpit or Meltonian Mel. If the test is unsuccessful, get professional advice from a good shoe shop.

on swimwear, beach towels and other washable fabrics Scrape carefully to remove as much surface deposit as possible. Hold an absorbent pad over the stain and dab it from below with cotton-wool moistened with eucalyptus oil. On non-rubberized items you can alternatively use a stain remover, such as Dabitoff, Polyclens Plus paint brush cleaner or Swarfega Hand Cleanser.

Tea

on blankets Rinse at once in warm water. If the mark has dried, try bleaching it carefully with hydrogen peroxide solution (1 part 20 vol peroxide to 6 parts cold water). Rinse and launder. On Acrilan blankets laundering may suffice.

on carpets Blot thoroughly. If the spill is recent, flush the area with a squirt from a soda syphon or sponge with warm water. When necessary, and where the tea contained milk, use a carpet shampoo. When dry, apply an aerosol stain remover such as Dabitoff if any traces remain. Dried tea stains should first be sponged with laundry borax solution (15 ml borax to 500 ml warm water). If marking remains, rub in a glycerine solution (equal parts glycerine and warm water), leave for up to an hour then rinse with clear water and use a carpet shampoo, following the manufacturer's instructions.

on non-washable fabrics and upholstery Sponge with a laundry borax solution (15 ml borax to 500 ml warm water) then with clear water. Blot well. When dry, use an aerosol stain remover, *eg*

Goddard's Dry Clean on any remaining traces. Alternatively, use an upholstery spotting kit (*see* ADDRESSES).

on table linen Rinse immediately under a cold tap. Clear traces by soaking and laundering, preferably in enzyme detergent solution, provided the fabric is suitable. Dried tea stains should be dampened, stretched over a basin, sprinkled with laundry borax powder and hot water poured through. Alternatively, treat whites with Dygon Colour and Stain Remover, or use a bleach solution on white cotton or linen without a crease-resistant or drip-dry finish. Launder.

on washable fabrics Rinse through in lukewarm water then soak in a laundry borax solution (15 ml borax to 500 ml warm water), or, if the fabric is suitable, in an enzyme detergent solution. Launder as usual. Dried stains should first be softened for an hour before washing with a glycerine solution (equal parts glycerine and warm water).

Tide marks *see* BATH STAINS.

Tobacco
on hands Rub neat Milton Sterilizing Fluid on to the stained areas with a pad of cotton-wool. Wash your hands in the usual way.

Tomato

juice *see* FRUIT JUICE.

ketchup *see* KETCHUP AND BOTTLED SAUCES.

purée *see* KETCHUP AND BOTTLED SAUCES.

Treacle *see* JAM.

Urine

on carpets Flush the area with a squirt from a soda syphon or sponge with cold water and blot well. Sponge the damp area with carpet shampoo solution. Rinse several times with cold water with a few drops of antiseptic added. Blot well each time. Where a dried stain has affected the dye, sponge with an ammonia solution (1.5 ml ammonia to 500 ml cold water).

on leather shoes Provided the urine is wiped off at once with a cloth lightly wrung out in warm water, no staining should remain. Buff gently. Where urine is allowed to dry out, rubbing with a damp cloth will achieve only superficial removal of the salts which have penetrated the leather. In this case, the treatment should be repeated from time to time as the perspiration from the foot gradually drives the salts to the surface.

on mattresses This is more easily done by two people as the mattress is best turned on its side and held in position while treatment is carried out. Press a towel below the stained area and sponge with a cold solution of washing-up liquid or upholstery shampoo. Wipe with cold water to which you have added a few drops of antiseptic, *eg* Dettol, Milton. Alternatively use an upholstery spotting kit (*see* ADDRESSES). It is probable that a ring mark will remain, but full treatment is nonetheless necessary both to remove the urine (which could cause the fabric to rot) and deodorize the area.

on non-washable fabrics Fresh stains should be sponged with cold water. Blot well. Sponge remaining stain with a vinegar solution (15 ml vinegar to 500 ml warm water). Dried stains require professional cleaning.

on suède shoes Penetration is rapid, so act quickly. Rub the marks lightly with a cloth well wrung out in warm water. Raise the suède nap by brushing while still damp with a suède brush. Dried marks may be difficult to remove but it is worth trying a suède and leather stain remover, such as Meltonian Stain Remover, which can be effective on water and salt staining.

Check first with safety rules on page 5

on washable bedding and fabrics   Rinse in cold water then launder as usual. Dried stains should first be soaked in an enzyme detergent solution (if the fabric is suitable). Marks on white and light fabrics (not nylon) can sometimes be bleached out with a hydrogen peroxide solution (1 part 20 vol peroxide to 6 parts cold water with a few drops of ammonia added).

Vodka   *see* GIN AND OTHER SPIRITS.

Vomit

on carpets   With the bowl of a spoon remove the deposit and flush the area with a squirt from a soda syphon. Blot well. Alternatively sponge the area with a laundry borax solution (15 ml borax to 500 ml warm water). Rub in the lather from a carpet shampoo solution. Repeat until stain has gone then rinse with warm water with a few drops of antiseptic added. Blot well. Alternatively, use a carpet spotting kit (*see* ADDRESSES) after removing the deposit.

on mattresses   Remove deposit and tip mattress on its side (*see also* URINE ON MATTRESSES). Sponge with a warm solution of washing-up liquid or upholstery shampoo such as Bissell Up-holstery Kit. Wipe over with cold water to which you have added a few drops of antiseptic. Blot well.

on non-washable fabrics   Spoon up the deposit. Delicate fabrics or expensive clothes should be dry-cleaned. Sponge the affected area with warm water to which you have added a few drops of ammonia. Blot dry. Alternatively use an upholstery spotting kit (*see* ADDRESSES).

on washable fabrics and bedding   Remove the surface deposit and rinse the area well under a running cold tap. If a suitable fabric, soak and launder in enzyme detergent solution, otherwise wash as usual.

Water marks

on wood   *see* PART 3, FURNITURE, REMOVING MARKS.

Whisky   *see* GIN AND OTHER SPIRITS.

Wine

on carpets   Flush the area with a squirt from a soda syphon or sponge with warm water. Blot well. Rub over area with carpet shampoo solution. Wipe with a cloth wrung out of clear water. Blot well. Repeat until clear. Alternatively use a carpet spotting kit (*see* ADDRESSES). A 50:50 solution of glycerine and water can be left on the stain for up to 1 hour to clear any remaining trace. Rinse off and blot well. Sponging with methylated spirit may reduce old stains.

on non-washable fabrics and upholstery Blot up as much as possible and sponge the area with warm clear water. Blot well. If a mark remains, sprinkle it with French chalk or talcum powder while still damp. Brush off after a few minutes and continue to repeat applications until clear. Dried stains may need lubricating with a glycerine solution (equal parts glycerine and warm water) left for 15 minutes then wiped with a cloth wrung out in warm detergent solution followed by clear water. Alternatively, use an upholstery spotting kit (*see* ADDRESSES).

on table linen White wine poured over a fresh red wine stain will neutralize it and make it easier to remove. Stretch the fabric over a bowl or basin and pour hot water through it. Otherwise rinse in warm water and soak in a laundry borax solution (15 ml borax to 500 ml warm water) or enzyme detergent solution before launder-

Check first with safety rules on page 5

ing as usual. Soak dried stains similarly. Dried stains on white fabrics should be stretched over a basin and sprinkled with laundry borax powder before hot water is poured through. Dygon Colour and Stain Remover will take out stubborn stains from white fabrics and a domestic bleach solution can be used on cottons and linens without easy care or drip-dry finishes.

on washable fabrics Rinse in warm water and if marks persist, soak or sponge in laundry borax solution (15 ml borax to 500 ml warm water) or enzyme detergent solution, where the fabric is suitable, before laundering. For dried marks on white wool or silk (but not nylon) bleach with a hydrogen peroxide solution (1 part 20 vol peroxide to 6 parts cold water). Rinse and launder. On other white fabrics use Dygon Colour and Stain Remover or a domestic bleach if the fabric has not a drip-dry or crease-resistant finish.

Xerox ink *see* DUPLICATING INKS.

3

Surfaces – and How to Care for Them

Regular, correct care of surfaces not only keeps them clean, hygienic and looking good, it also prevents the build-up of many of the stains referred to in Part 2. This section describes the general care needed for cleaning not only various types of surface but also a number of particular items that are likely to be found in many homes.

Acrylic

Baths, basins and shower trays If these are rinsed with warm soapy water and left as dry as possible after use, regular cleaning is made considerably easier. Clean and treat for stains and scratches as described under BATHS.

Furniture Little special care is required for acrylic (rigid plastic) furniture. Regular wiping over with a soft cloth or sponge dampened in a weak detergent solution (use washing-up liquid) followed by rinsing will not only keep it clean but reduce the build-up of static and stop the furniture from attracting dust.

Slight scratching may cause dullness but this can often be removed by rubbing with a soft cloth moistened with a metal polish such as Brasso or Silvo. Stains, too, can often be removed in this way. Wipe off with a moist cloth and buff well. Deeper scratches will need to be rubbed out with fine grade glass paper and finished off with the finest grade wet or dry abrasive paper. Afterwards polish with a metal polish.

Utensils Wipe or wash with a soft cloth or sponge dampened in a weak detergent solution as for ACRYLIC FURNITURE above. Clean kitchen utensils quickly as staining can occur easily. Some stains can be removed with a non-abrasive kitchen cleaner or a damp cloth dipped in bicarbonate of soda.

Alabaster

Alabaster is porous and should never be immersed in water but just wiped over with a chamois leather wrung out in a solution of washing-up detergent to remove surface soiling. Discolouration— for example, nicotine stains in an ash-tray—should be wiped with a cloth moistened very sparingly with turpentine (the real thing, not white spirit). Buff well with a soft clean cloth or chamois leather. Heavy marking may respond to professional polishing.

Aluminium
Cooking pans Wash, as soon as possible after use, with hot water and washing-up liquid, using a nylon washing-up brush or scouring pad, such as Scotchbrite, to loosen any food deposit. A steel wool soap pad, such as Brillo, or fine steel wool can be used from time to time to burnish the surface, but rinse thoroughly afterwards as particles of steel wool left in contact with the aluminium can cause surface pitting. Non-stick surfaces or mirror-finished aluminium should never be treated with abrasives.

To remove the discolouration that occurs from boiling water, boil up a weak acid solution in the pan (use water plus lemon skin, apple parings or rhubarb), rinse and dry. Never leave food overnight in an aluminium pan as it can cause the surface to pit irrevocably. 15 ml of laundry borax in the washing-up water will help to clean aluminium cookware and soaking in a laundry borax solution (15 ml borax to 500 ml water) will often remove stains.

ANODIZED ALUMINIUM
Light fittings, trays, trolleys, *etc* made of anodized aluminium should simply be wiped clean with a damp cloth. A little liquid wax polish on a dry cloth will maintain their gleam. Never use abrasives on them. Anodized saucepan lids can be washed up in the usual way, but they should not be put into a dishwasher. Avoid the use of abrasive cleaners.

Teapots The stained interior of an aluminium teapot can be cleaned by filling with hot water, adding 15 ml washing powder and leaving for an hour or two. Alternatively use a proprietary stain remover such as Chempro T, avoiding spillage on the outside of the pot. Then brush the inside well with a bottle brush or old (well-cleaned) toothbrush and rinse thoroughly.

Antique furniture
Should you be so lucky as to own some of this, you'll find that its worst enemies are modern developments like central heating. You can mitigate against its effects somewhat by keeping the heating at a constant level of around 18°C (65°F); by avoiding standing valuable pieces near radiators or by keeping them in rooms where the heating isn't on a great deal. The use of a humidifier will also help to prevent the wood drying out too much.

Keeping the finish of antique furniture in good condition doesn't require as much elbow grease as you might imagine. Experts tend to think that it is not a good idea to use modern furniture polishes with added silicones on antique pieces because they tend to give an unnatural finish. Good non-silicone polishes include Renaissance Wax Polish (*see* ADDRESSES), Goddard's Cabinet Maker's Wax, Antiquax and Kleeneze Antique Furniture Polish. You can also make your own from 50 g beeswax, shredded into a jam jar, plus 125 ml pure turpentine. Stand the jar in hot water until the wax melts to form a buttery paste (do not heat it on the cooker—turpentine is highly flammable). Screw a lid on the jar and use sparingly when required.

Dust antique furniture regularly and remove any greasy marks with a chamois leather which has been well wrung out in a solution of vinegar and water (1 part vinegar to 8 parts water). Buff with a soft cloth until absolutely dry, then polish as usual

For the removal of more serious marks, *eg* burns, scratches, water marks *etc*, from antique furniture it is best to seek professional advice. However, for a list of such marks, together with instructions on how they may be removed, *see* FURNITURE.

Note For the removal of *any* marks from French-polished furniture *see* FRENCH-POLISHED SURFACES.

Arborite *see* LAMINATED PLASTIC SURFACES.

Asbestos

In spite of alarmist attitudes, asbestos is a perfectly safe material to have in the home provided it is handled correctly. It should never on any account be scraped or cut as it is the small particles which *can* cause health hazards. It should also never be sponged or immersed in water as this softens it and makes the surface break up.

Iron stands Should be wiped lightly with a damp cloth to remove surface soiling. Scorch marks should simply be left and no attempt made to remove them by scraping or abrading.

Heat diffuser mats These are used on cooker tops and should be wiped with a damp cloth to remove spillage. Badly stained or flaking mats should be thrown out.

Baking tins

Badly neglected and greasy tins (except aluminium or non-stick ones) should be boiled up with a strong washing soda solution in a large old pan, then rinsed and dried.

For cleaning advice on aluminium baking tins *see* ALUMINIUM COOKING PANS. Ordinary 'tin' baking tins need washing from time to time though the less often they're washed, the more quickly a non-stick patina is likely to build up. Try just wiping them out with kitchen paper unless you have cooked something like chocolate or treacle cake which tends to stick and needs very thorough greasing of the tins. When they have to be washed, avoid harsh abrasives which damage the coating. After washing, dry them at once or they will rust. A good way to do this is to pop them in the cooling oven.

Bamboo

Use a brush or preferably a vacuum cleaner attachment to keep bamboo free of dust. When noticeably dirty, clean it by scrubbing gently with warm soapy water (don't use a synthetic detergent) with 5 ml laundry borax added to each 500 ml. Rinse this off with warm salted water (10 ml salt to 1 litre water) to help both stiffen it up and bleach it. Wipe with a cloth and allow it to dry naturally, outdoors if at all possible. Polish with furniture cream.

Non-stick bakeware Should be washed thoroughly taking care not to use a sharp implement or harsh abrasives which might damage the surface. Follow any specific cleaning instructions. Allow it to dry before storing. Gold-coloured bakeware should be washed in clear water and *no* detergent which would damage the surface; again, follow the individual manufacturer's advice.

Basketware and cane

Try to avoid allowing basketware or cane to become very dirty as it is difficult to get thoroughly clean again. Use a soft brush to remove dust and light soiling. Very dirty sections of unvarnished cane can be rubbed with fine steel wool dipped into a solution of warm water and a little washing soda. Slightly dirty cane should be wiped down with this solution then with cold water to firm it up.

Take care not to over-wet the cane. Wipe with a cloth and leave to dry naturally so that it does not warp. Some cane furniture has a clear or coloured varnish finish. This just needs wiping over with a damp cloth from time to time.

Baths

Different types of bath require different care. New baths will normally come with instructions for this which should be followed exactly. All baths will need little special care provided they are rinsed immediately after use with warm soapy water and wiped dry. A daily clean with neat washing-up liquid on a damp cloth or sponge followed by rinsing will do the rest.

Acrylic baths These should not present problems if they are correctly cleaned from the start. Always rinse out well after use, and if necessary wipe the surface with a cloth or bath cleaning sponge, moistened with neat washing-up liquid or rubbed on a cake of soap. Bear in mind when choosing that dark colours are more likely to show up deposits and staining.

Light scratches can be removed by rubbing gently with Silvo. In the case of deeper scratches or difficult stains, the surface should be lightly rubbed with a very fine grade of wet or dry abrasive paper, always using it wet, and working with progressively finer grades of wet or dry, or using the same piece which gradually becomes worn away. Finish by rubbing with metal polish *eg* Silvo.

Bath preparations such as foam baths, bath cubes, etc., are not usually recommended as deposits may remain on the surface after the bath has been emptied, and these soda or acidic deposits can damage the bath.

Glass fibre baths These need special care since the colour is in the form of a surface coating of a 'gel' or 'resin'. If abrasives, even one as fine as Silvo, are constantly used on these they may remove the colour completely, leaving a white patch.

Vitreous and porcelain enamelled baths Use a proprietary bath cleaner such as Jif. Gumption Bathroom Cream Cleanser, Cleen-o-Pine Cream, Izal Bath Cleaner or Flash. Harsh abrasives should be avoided as they will eventually dull the surface of the bath and make it harder to clean.

Blankets

With correct care, blankets should last for many years. If you can

Check first with safety rules on page 5

'rest' them from time to time, stored properly, you will lengthen their useful life. Any blankets not in use should be washed or cleaned then aired and sealed in a polythene bag and placed in a cool cupboard where they won't be crushed. Unless they have been permanently treated against moths, wool and wool mixture blankets should include a moth-repellent sachet in the bag. New blankets will carry a label or swing ticket saying how they should be cleaned.

Many natural and synthetic fibre blankets can be washed, either by hand or in a washing machine. Before embarking on this, it is sensible to check whether the dry blanket will actually fit in your washing machine (and also in the spin dryer in the case of a twin-tub). It may be more sensible to use a local laundrette with larger machines since the weight of some blankets could unbalance a smaller domestic model. If you're going to hand wash, using the bath or a large sink, do bear in mind that something like a double blanket becomes an almost unmanageable mass when wet.

Professional cleaning is the alternative and is specially recommended in any case for some blankets. Some laundries and dry-cleaners operate special blanket washing and cleaning services and it's best to use these. Local addresses are available from the Association of British Launderers and Cleaners Ltd., Lancaster Gate House, 319 Pinner Road, Harrow, Middx HA1 4HX. It is not recommended to dry-clean blankets in a coin-op machine, as they must be aired very thoroughly before they are replaced on a bed since any fumes remaining in them are toxic.

Electric   Some electric blankets are washable; the manufacturer's instructions for washing should be followed. Never use an electric blanket until it is completely dry. Where an electric blanket has to be dry-cleaned it must usually be returned to the maker who will service it at the same time. This should be done regularly—every three years is the recommended time but check the instructions.

Books

Books need regular dusting to keep them in good condition. When removing one from a bookcase after a period of time, always blow along the top or wipe it with a soft cloth to prevent dust falling down between the pages. All books should be either dusted with a feather duster or gone over with a vacuum cleaner attachment once a year whether they've been read or not.

Leather-bound books need special treatment to stop them cracking. Wipe them from time to time with a cloth well wrung out in a warm glycerine-soap solution (whisk soap tablet in warm water give a lather) then apply hide food, *eg* Connolly's Cee Bee Hide Food, while still damp. Alternatively use Fortificuir (*see* ADDRESSES), a special dressing which both cleans and preserves— follow the maker's instructions. Valuable books may need professional treatment for bookworm or mildew, in which case seek advice from your local specialist bookseller or museum.

Bookshelves

Dust regularly and treat according to the material they are made of. Do not allow sticky polish to build up on the shelves and get transferred to the books. Where books have got bookworm, treat the shelves too with a good insecticidal spray and polish with an anti-woodworm polish.

Boots *see* LEATHER, SHOES for general care.

Brass

Brass is a copper alloy which tarnishes easily. To clean it use either a metal polish such as Brasso or Duraglit Wadding Metal Polish. Ornamental brass will benefit from the tarnish-reducing film put on it by a long-term polish such as Goddard's Long Term Brass and Copper Polish. A home-made cleaner which gives good results is a mixture of equal quantities of vinegar, salt and flour made into a paste. Rub this on then wash it off in hot soapy water. Rinse and buff with a soft cloth. Lacquered brass may become discoloured under the lacquer finish. In this case, remove the finish with either cellulose thinners or nail varnish remover (both highly flammable). Then clean.

Neglected and corroded items should be treated with spirits of salts (a **poisonous** and **corrosive** acid). Wear rubber gloves and work in a well-ventilated place, protecting the work surface. Rub on with a rag tied on the end of a stick. Rinse off in several bowls of clean water. If green corrosion does not respond to this, it should be soaked overnight in a solution of washing soda and hot water (a handful to a washing-up bowlful), then rinsed, dried and polished. Salt and lemon juice mixed to a paste will clean up slightly neglected items.

Brick flooring

To clean brick flooring use a solution of washing-up detergent and scrub with a stiff-bristled brush. Flash can be used on a heavily soiled surface. Avoid soap, which produces a white crystal-

Check first with safety rules on page 5

line deposit. Mop up the detergent solution, rinse with clear water and wipe as dry as possible. Try to use as little water as possible since an excess brings soluble salts to the surface of the bricks and also lengthens the drying time. Porous brick floors are easier to clean if they are first sealed with a sealer such as Bourneseal. For the care of brick fireplaces, *see* FIREPLACES.

Bronze

For regular cleaning, bronze just needs dusting. The occasional application of a very small quantity of oil or brown-coloured shoe polish followed by buffing will improve the sheen and also help prevent the appearance of the characteristic green spots. Badly soiled bronze can be washed in hot soapy water or rubbed over with pure turps or paraffin (both flammable). When dry, brush it with stiff (not wire) brush that will not scratch the surface.

Brushes

Brooms and cleaning brushes These pick up a lot of dirt. Remove this regularly—wear household gloves and pick out the larger particles by hand. Wash in a warm mild detergent solution with final rinse in cold water to stiffen the bristles, then hang up to dry. Do not store brooms and brushes so that they rest on their bristles as this flattens them and destroys their effectiveness. Many come supplied with a hanging hook, if not it is an easy matter to make one by screwing a cup hook into the top of the handle.

Hair brushes With a comb, remove loose hairs after use. Wash every time you wash your hair by beating up and down gently in warm soapy water. The ventilation hole in a rubber-based brush should be plugged with a small piece of paper or a matchstick before washing. Rinse finally in cold water to stiffen the bristles. Allow the brush to dry naturally away from artificial heat, preferably hanging on a string, otherwise tipped on its side. Do not wet the back of the brush unless plastic—wooden backs tend to swell and ivory and tortoiseshell backs could be damaged irreparably. For special care of ivory and tortoiseshell-backed brushes, *see* IVORY and TORTOISESHELL.

Paint brushes Clean according to what paint you have been using—the instructions are usually provided on the tin. Some of the newer oil-based paints can be cleared with water and washing-up liquid or a solution of powder detergent—otherwise white spirit or a proprietary paint brush cleaner will be needed. Use cold water to remove emulsion paint from brushes. If soaking is required, do not stand them directly on their bristles but drill a hole through the handle and suspend them in the liquid from a taut string or nail. There is no need to clean brushes if you are just stopping painting for a short time. Just wrap the bristles tightly in aluminium foil until the brush is next required.

Cane *see* BASKETWARE AND CANE.

Canvas

Blinds Scrub with washing soap and warm water or a synthetic detergent solution, then rinse thoroughly in cold water. Allow to dry naturally, outdoors if possible, and try to avoid making a crease by hanging the blind over two parallel lines.

Garden furniture *see* GARDEN FURNITURE.

Handbags Wipe over with a damp cloth and allow to dry naturally. If really soiled, scrub with a nailbrush and soap lather. Scrape off any residual foam with the back of a knife, then wipe over with a damp cloth. Do not over-wet. Allow to dry naturally.

Tents Only clean if absolutely essential. Tents have a tough, resilient, water-proof coating which will protect against mildew for up to 3 days if you have to fold your tent and steal away without actually having time to dry it thoroughly. When dirty, brush off dirt and any mildew. If washing is essential use a detergent solution and rinse several times to ensure none remains in the fabric, otherwise reproofing won't work. Reproof only if necessary, using NEV for cotton canvases and Fabsil silicone waterproofer for synthetics (*see* ADDRESSES). Most tents will withstand winter storage with just a thorough brushing and airing.

Carpets

GENERAL CARE

Carpets are among the most expensive items when it comes to fitting out a home, so it makes sense to care for them well. Most new carpets come supplied with care instructions. If these are not available ask a reliable retailer or write to the carpet manufacturer to ensure that any treatment you do yourself is of the right kind and will not damage the carpet in any way. RUSH MATTING and SISAL MATTING are dealt with under separate headings.

Check first with safety rules on page 5

Try to avoid disturbing a carpet that has recently been laid any more than is absolutely necessary; a good rule to follow is that new carpets should be left to settle for a few weeks after laying and lightly vacuumed or brushed gently by hand, in the direction of the pile, to remove the fluff. After this it is essential to vacuum them regularly so as to remove embedded dust and grit and to keep the pile in good condition. Long or 'shag' pile carpets are more difficult to clean and will need regular attention with a carpet rake (available from good carpet retailers). This can be used for lifting the pile to free loose soiling before vacuuming, as well as tidying it after vacuuming. A cylinder cleaner is more effective on 'shag' pile than the upright type. Spots and spills should be removed from carpets as soon as possible after they occur (*see* PART 2 for specific stains).

Cleaning When overall cleaning becomes necessary, there are various methods which can be carried out at home; the carpet can be sent to professional cleaners, or you can call in professional cleaners to deal with a carpet *in situ. In situ* cleaning is usually preferable for fitted carpets since shrinkage is less likely to occur due to the carpet fixings holding them taut.

Home cleaning can be done either by applying the lather from a solution of dry foam shampoo such as 1001 Dri-foam or Bissell Carpet Shampoo or by the 'steam' method. Dry foam shampoo can be applied using a sponge (which is tiring), by a hand-operated applicator (which is also fairly tiring) or by an electric shampooer which looks rather like a vacuum cleaner and dispenses measured amounts of shampoo at the lift of a lever—these can either be bought or hired by the day. Steam cleaners are hired (or you can pay someone to use one in your home). They do not in fact work by steaming but by spraying hot water and a cleansing agent, under pressure, into the carpet pile then extracting it immediately together with any dirt lodged in the carpet. This is a very effective method of carpet cleaning but more expensive than dry foam shampooing and also more tiring to do if you are operating the machine yourself.

It is important when cleaning a carpet not to over-wet it or colour may come through from the backing and the backing itself may distort. Deep pile carpets may need more than one application. Ideally all furniture should be removed from the room but if it has to be put back before the carpet is completely dry, put small pieces of aluminium foil under any parts that touch the carpet to prevent marks forming.

Cast iron

Cookware Wash thoroughly and dry immediately to prevent rust forming. Use steel wool or a Brillo pad. Rinse thoroughly.

Decorative ware Decorative ware without a protective coating should first have any rust loosened with a wire brush or steel wool. Wear goggles to prevent particles flying in your eyes. If necessary use a rust remover such as Jenolite, following the maker's instructions. On embossed and engraved surfaces watch that a heavy brush does not damage the surface. To prevent further rusting, apply a thin layer of oil or a film of petroleum jelly. Alternatively use boot polish or a paste wax furniture polish.

Ceilings and walls

Ceilings need attention less frequently than walls although the treatment for both is the same. To clean painted surfaces *see* EGGSHELL, EMULSION AND GLOSS PAINT. To clean vinyl wall coverings *see* VINYL; to clean wallpaper *see* WALLPAPER. To clean or prepare for re-painting first dust the ceiling using a special brush or the brush attachment of a vacuum cleaner. Wash over any dirty parts with a soft scrubbing brush and warm solution of washing-up liquid, then wipe over the whole ceiling with a cloth wrung out in the solution. Wipe over again with a cloth wrung out in clean water and ensure that all traces of detergent are removed. Use this treatment on tobacco smoke stains, water stains and the heat marks that appear above radiators and chimney breasts prior to painting with emulsion paint. If you are going to put oil-based paint on the ceiling, clean it as described, allow to dry then prime with an aluminium primer or sealer before painting.

Cement and concrete

Wash with a detergent solution or a cupful of washing soda dissolved in a bucket of warm water. Cement and concrete floors are best sealed for easy cleaning. After washing thoroughly, remove any ingrained grease marks with Bell 1966 Cleaner, rinse off and let it dry thoroughly. Seal with Bourneseal.

Ceramic tiles *see* FIREPLACES; FLOORS; TILED SURFACES.

Chandeliers

If possible, chandeliers should be removed from their hanging position for cleaning so that you can handle each piece of glass

Check first with safety rules on page 5

separately. Use a soft, non-fluffy cloth, preferably fine linen, wrung out in Handy Andy or a solution of washing-up liquid, plus a few drops of ammonia. Rinse, dry and polish each piece with another dry cloth before reassembling. A laborious but effective method of cleaning a chandelier is to rub all over the facets wearing dry chamois leather gloves.

China, bone

Fine bone china is best washed by hand unless it is specifically marked dishwasher-proof. Use a weak, warm (not hot) solution of washing-up liquid with a soft brush, cloth or mop. Avoid scouring pads, harsh abrasives, bleach or soda which can damage the surface or dull the pattern, especially gold or silver decoration. Use a plastic washing-up bowl in the sink to prevent knocking china on the sink itself. After washing rinse each piece in clear warm water, drain, then dry and polish with a soft tea towel. Do not stack wet pieces on top of each other while draining—a plastic-coated wire rack is a good holder for them. Watch whether any acids such as vinegar or fruit juice seem to affect your china (usually it is the colour that changes) and always wash any pieces so affected immediately. Use a cold water rinse to loosen egg staining and rub over with a damp cloth dipped in salt if it's difficult to get off.

Chromium plate

This is mainly found on taps in the home and on some tubular furniture. Never use steel wool or an abrasive on it as this will damage the thin plating. Wash or wipe with a cloth moistened in mild detergent solution, rinse and buff. Marks should be rubbed with a damp cloth dipped in bicarbonate of soda. Treat corrosion with a metal cleaner such as Silvo, Duraglit Silver Polish impregnated wadding, or Three-in-One Chrome Cleaner (from car accessory shops).

Concrete   *see* CEMENT AND CONCRETE.

Continental quilts   *see* DUVETS.

Cookers

New cookers come with the manufacturer's recommended instructions for cleaning the various parts and it is sensible to hang on to these and follow them as necessary. One good way to keep a cooker clean is to prevent it ever becoming very dirty. Always wipe up spills and splashes on the hob or in the oven as soon as is practicable, preferably while the surface is still warm and the spill has not become hard. For more major cleaning you should first either turn off the electricity at the cooker box or extinguish the pilot light(s).

Electric cookers It is not usually necessary to clean radiant rings or solid plates as these burn themselves clean during use. It is important though, and especially on electric ceramic hobs, to wipe up all spills as they occur to stop them hardening or burning on. With ceramic hobs, use the manufacturer's recommended cleaner. Clean non-ceramic hobs, the back splash and spillage trays with a damp cloth and washing-up liquid solution and wipe dry. Marks should be removed according to the material the surface is made from—*see* ENAMEL and STAINLESS STEEL. The grill should burn off any grease during cooking. Use a soft dry brush on residual soiling and wash a removable grill cover in hot washing-up liquid solution in the sink.

Gas cookers Wash all removable parts in hot washing-up liquid solution in the sink, using a nylon cleaning pad to remove encrusted dirt. Where possible, soak stubborn marks and rub off with a soap-impregnated steel wool pad or a mild abrasive cleaner. Clean the hob itself, back splash, spillage trays and grill as for electric cookers.

Ovens How you clean an oven will depend on its internal finish. Continuous cleaning linings work by vaporizing fat splashes during cooking so that they do not become deposited. The oven needs to be fairly hot to do this effectively so you should try to cook at a high temperature every so often to give the oven a good clean. If necessary the linings can be wiped with a damp cloth. Heavy spillage may fall on to the oven base and needs to be wiped up as soon as cooking is finished. Don't use any form of abrasive cleaner on a non-stick base. High temperature cleaning ovens are found on some electric cookers and the manufacturers' instructions should be followed carefully.

Vitreous enamel oven linings should be cleaned with a liquid or paste cleaner made for use on this surface. For heavy soiling use an impregnated oven-cleaning pad or paste or gel oven cleaner that has been approved by the Vitreous Enamel Development Council (*see* ADDRESSES). Follow the instructions supplied with the cleaner, being careful not to let it touch continuous clean or non-stick surfaces. Work in a well ventilated atmosphere and wear rubber gloves. Clean the oven shelves with a nylon cleaning pad in hot washing-up liquid solution.

Check first with safety rules on page 5

Glass oven doors These can usually be removed for easier clean-ing at the sink. Use a nylon cleaning pad and, on stubborn marks, a paste or liquid household cleaner as well. Avoid steel wool which could scratch the glass. Do not use an aerosol oven cleaner which could cause the warm glass to disintegrate through thermal shock.

Copper

For the general care of copper, *see* BRASS. Copper saucepans should have their exteriors cleaned with vinegar and salt, or a proprietary cleaner such as Duraglit Wadding Metal Polish. They will be lined with either tin or nickel as copper reacts adversely with certain foods and from time to time the lining will need renewing.

Corduroy *see* VELVET.

Cork *see* FLOORS.

Cowhide *see* LEATHER.

Curtain rails, plastic

Remove dust from curtain headings and rails at regular invervals using the suction nozzle of your vacuum cleaner. When curtains are removed for cleaning or washing, wipe down the tracks with a cloth wrung out in a warm solution of washing-up liquid followed by clear warm water. The best results are obtained if the rails can be lifted down and washed or rinsed in a bath since an old toothbrush can then be used to clear the channel of accumulated dust and flies. This is easier if you remove the gliders and soak them separately in a basin of the solution, followed by rinsing. Take care to protect the bottom of the bath with a cloth or an old towel to prevent scratching and try to wet any curtain cords as little as possible; otherwise shrinkage may occur.

If the gliders stick, although apparently free from obstruction, carefully spray the channel with an aerosol lubricant such as Rocket WD40 (don't get it on the curtains). Do not use polish which leaves a sticky surface.

Curtains

Whether curtains should be washed or dry-cleaned depends in theory on the fabric from which they are made. In practice, it is often impracticable to wash even washable curtains at home as their bulk when wet makes them unmanageable and difficult to dry and iron satisfactorily. To keep major cleaning of curtains to a minimum it is important to dust them down regularly using either the brush attachment of a vacuum cleaner or a soft, long-handled brush. Hanging them outside on a fine, breezy day will help to freshen them up from time to time. Lining curtains helps to prevent dirt, condensation and fading from sunlight affecting the main fabric (apart from affording a greater degree of privacy). As a rough guide, fabrics which can be washed include cottons, linens, man-made fibres and most sheers. Those which should be dry-cleaned include the mixtures of man-made fibres, silks, wool sheers, most pile fabrics and other heavy materials.

When washing curtains at home follow any laundering instructions supplied. Remove all the hooks and curtain weights and loosen the curtain heading tapes. Shake them outside to remove dust, or lay them on the floor and run a vacuum cleaner attachment over them. A cold water soak prior to laundering will get rid of a fair amount of soiling. Suit the wash water temperature to the

Check first with safety rules on page 5

fabric, make sure the detergent is thoroughly dissolved before putting in the curtains, and do not rub or wring. If you are machine washing, follow the wash programme for the most delicate fibre involved. Thorough rinsing is essential for good results. Squeeze out as much water as possible (some fabrics can be spin dried) and hang the curtains over two parallel lines to avoid strain on the fabric.

Iron, when necessary, while still slightly damp, working lengthwise on the wrong side. You will need to stretch the curtains gently into shape as you go to avoid puckering along the seams. If a synthetic fabric has become too dry for ironing, it is better to damp it down completely, as sprinkling is likely to leave spot marks. Take the opportunity to clean the windows and sills thoroughly before re-hanging the curtains. When curtains are taken for dry cleaning, tell the cleaner, if possible, the type of fabric concerned.

It is important to wash net curtains before they begin to look grubby, otherwise they become permanently discoloured. Wash separately from other articles and do not exceed the recommended washing and drying temperatures, or permanent creasing will result.

Decanters and carafes

Decanters and carafes become stained and cloudy either because wine is left in them or because they are put away when damp. If the glass has become etched there is nothing you can do to remove the marks. Otherwise they can be cleaned either by filling with a warm solution of enzyme detergent and leaving to soak, or by pouring in a mixture of vinegar and salt (125 ml vinegar to 15 ml salt) and shaking from time to time. After both methods, you should rinse the decanter thoroughly in warm (not hot) water and stand it upside down in a wide-necked jug to drain and become thoroughly dry before being stored. Very bad marks will sometimes respond to soaking in a proprietary stain remover for tableware such as Chempro T.

Diamonds *see* JEWELLERY.

Duvets

To keep a duvet clean, always use a coverslip to protect it from the sleeper and also from dirt and spillage. You can buy coverslips or make your own; most people prefer those made from a cotton or a mixture of natural and man-made fibres since completely synthetic ones tend to be very hot and also to slip around.

Wash coverslips according to the fabric they are made of—a label should specify this. Deep-dyed coverslips should be washed separately from other laundry until you are sure that no colour runs from them.

Spills on duvets should be mopped immediately to stop them sinking in. If the cover is soiled, push the filling down its channel and tie a piece of white string or cord around the section. Treat according to the type of stain—*see* PART 2. Duvets with synthetic fibre fillings can be washed. This is difficult to do at home as the wet mass is large and unmanageable. It is better to use a laundrette which has larger machines or to have it professionally laundered. Washing duvets is not likely to improve the texture of the filling and should be done as infrequently as possible.

Although some duvets with natural fillings can be washed, most require dry-cleaning. This should only be done by specialist duvet cleaners and *never* in a coin-op machine because of the danger of toxic fumes not being thoroughly aired out of the filling.

For general day to day care, give a duvet a good shake each time

Check first with safety rules on page 5

you make the bed to keep the filling evenly distributed. Turn it over and from top to bottom from time to time to even out wear. On fine days put it over a washing line or out of a window to allow fresh air to circulate in it.

Earthenware

Earthenware is one of the more common forms of tableware. True earthenware is opaque and, in spite of its sturdier appearance, not as hard nor as resistant to chipping and breaking as bone china. Underneath the glaze it is porous so cracked earthenware will absorb liquids. Some earthenware is ovenproof and usually labelled accordingly, but most tableware should be warmed gently, not placed in a hot oven. Only some types of earthenware can be washed in a dishwasher; they are labelled accordingly. Provided the glaze is not damaged, burnt or stuck-on food will come off after soaking.

Ebony

Never wash ebony as this can damage it. Use a duster to remove surface soiling. Rubbing with a clean cloth regularly and the occasional application of a little furniture cream will keep it in good condition.

Eggshell, emulsion and gloss paint

To clean, first dust the painted area with a soft brush or cloth. Use the brush attachment on your vacuum cleaner or a duster tied over a broom or mop head to reach the higher areas. Using a warm but well diluted solution of washing-up liquid, wash the wall, working from the bottom to the top. This means that any dirty streaks which roll down will reach a clean surface from which they can be wiped easily. Dirt on dirt is much harder to remove. Never use a washing powder as these contain fluorescers which make your washing look brighter but can alter the colour of paint.

Heavily soiled walls should be washed with a weak solution of sugar soap or diluted general purpose household cleaner. Really dirty patches can be removed with neat general purpose household cleaner. After washing, rinse with clear water using an absorbent sponge or cloth. Work in small areas, washing and rinsing each one before you move on to the next. Do not stop until you have completed a whole wall or you will create a line which is difficult to remove.

Note Turn off the electricity at the mains before washing around electrical sockets and light switches.

Electric blankets *see* BLANKETS, ELECTRIC.

Embroidery
If an embroidered article needs cleaning, seek advice from a good dry-cleaner, or the textile department of a museum, depending on its quality.

Emulsion paint *see* EGGSHELL, EMULSION AND GLOSS PAINT.

Enamel
Stoved enamel Usually found on the cabinets (but not always the tops) of appliances such as washing machines, fridges and freezers. These can be kept clean by regular spraying with a cleaner/polish such as Sparkle which you then wipe off. Greasy surfaces can be washed first, using a hot detergent solution. Never polish inside any appliance.

Vitreous enamel Found on baths, cooker hobs, oven interiors and the worktops of some appliances. It is glass fused to metal and is more durable than stoved enamel. It can however be scratched with harsh abrasives. To clean vitreous enamel, wash it regularly with a cloth wrung out in detergent solution. Attack marks with a cleaning product such as Flash, Ajax or Jif. Really stubborn marks may need the use of a special product such as RB70 stain and scale remover (*see* ADDRESSES).

Enamelware
Small items with an enamel coating are called enamelware—things like saucepans, colanders, jugs, mugs and teapots. The enamel may be the vitreous type (see above) or simply a sprayed on polyimide finish. Normal washing-up should keep these items clean; in hard water areas it is important to dry them immediately to prevent whitish film forming on the surface. Marks can be removed with Jif, Ajax, Flash or any other cleaner recommended by the Vitreous Enamel Development Council (*see* ADDRESSES). Keep to a cream cleaner such as Jif on a polyimide finish. Stained pan interiors will come clean after soaking in a mild solution of household bleach (5 ml to 500 ml water). *See* also COOKERS AND PANS.

Fabrics *see* PART 4.

Felt
Felt is very difficult to clean as its dyes are unstable, so water

---

and water-based products like carpet shampoo cannot be used. Felt can be dry-cleaned satisfactorily in a 100% spirit solution but after a couple of times it will begin to look shabby. In any case most dry-cleaners use some water in their solutions. Liquid solvents can be used to remove dirty marks but tend to leave rings or clean patches. The best way to care for felt is to ensure it does not get dirty (line curtains, for example, to reduce soiling). General cleaning can be done with the upholstery tool of a vacuum cleaner and marks are best removed with a soft-bristled or special suède brush.

Fibre glass *see* GLASS FIBRE.

Fire irons *see* BRASS, COPPER or CAST IRON according to the material the fire irons are made of.

Fireplaces
Wherever possible keep to the fireplace manufacturers' cleaning instructions.

Brick With a vacuum cleaner attachment or soft brush remove dust and soot from the brick and then scrub with a hard scrubbing brush and clear warm water. If soiling does not respond, or there are burn marks, try washing down with malt vinegar followed by thorough rinsing.

To remove heavy soot staining *see* PART 2, SMOKE AND SOOT.

Cast iron Remove loose rust scaling with a wire brush or steel wool (wear goggles to protect your eyes), taking care not to brush so hard that embossed or engraved surfaces are damaged. Remove any further rust with a proprietary product such as Jenolite Rust Remover following the manufacturer's instructions for applying and neutralizing. To prevent further rusting, it is a good idea to apply a thin layer of oil.

Ceramic tile Wash over the tiles with warm soapy water or a solution of washing-up liquid. If necessary, use a fine paste cleaner, such as Chemico, but not a highly abrasive one nor a harsh brush which could damage the glaze. (Never apply a damp cloth to the tiles while they are still hot as this could cause cracking.) When dry, give a light application of furniture polish such as Mr Sheen or a furniture cream, *eg* Min, and rub well with a soft duster or clean, dry cloth.

Marble Sponge or scrub with clear warm water. Polished marble should be cleaned with Bell 1967 Cleaner and polished with Bell Marble Polish. Worn marble can be improved with Bell Special Marble Cleaner. Chipped or damaged areas can be repaired with Bell Marble 'Touch Up' Pack (*see* ADDRESSES).

Riven slate Scrub with a stiff-bristled brush dipped into washing-up liquid solution. Follow the manufacturer's advice on stain removal.

Stone Sponge light soiling with clear warm water. Use a scrubbing brush if necessary to remove ingrained particles. For heavier soiling add a little washing-up liquid to the cleaning water then rinse the area thoroughly. Do not use soap or scouring powder which can affect the colour. On badly soiled fireplaces scrub with a strong solution of domestic bleach but take care to protect the surround. In cases of really bad marking it is sensible to consult the fireplace manufacturer about cleaning.

Floors
Different types of flooring need different care. Basic floor care includes having door mats by all exterior doors to prevent dirt

Check first with safety rules on page 5

being brought into the home, vacuuming or sweeping up loose dirt regularly and always before applying polish, washing regularly where necessary, applying the minimum amount of polish to produce a good shine, removing polish build-up when it starts to get tacky. Where possible, always follow the manufacturer's instructions for maintenance.

Ceramic tiles merely need regular cleaning with a floor mop or cloth wrung out in hot washing-up liquid solution. Rinse with clear water then buff with a soft cloth tied round a mop or broom head. Dirty grouting between ceramic tiles should be cleaned with a soft bristled brush. Never apply polish as this makes the tiles slippery.

Cork should have a sealed or waxed finish or vinyl coating to prevent dirt becoming embedded in the otherwise porous surface. Sealed cork just needs damp mopping and the occasional light application of emulsion polish. Waxed cork needs occasional applications of liquid or paste wax polish such as Furmoto or Johnson Wax. If the finish becomes water marked, rub the marks with a cloth dipped in liquid wax polish. Vinyl-coated cork needs regular damp mopping and very infrequent applications of emulsion polish, *eg* Johnson Klear.

Linoleum Use a floor mop dampened in a weak solution of general purpose household cleaner and do not over-wet. Once dry, use a liquid or wax paste polish, *eg* Johnson Beautiflor Liquid Wax or Mansion Wax. In kitchens and bathrooms use emulsion polish instead, *eg* Johnson Klear, as this does not water mark. To remove scuff marks, rub with a cloth moistened in polish.

Quarry tiles Glazed quarry tiles just need mopping with water to which you have added a little liquid general purpose cleaner, such as Ajax. Unglazed tiles will need scrubbing with this solution to remove dirt. Rinse and wipe dry. Unglazed tiles then need to be polished with a liquid or paste wax polish (preferably the non-slip type such as Furmoto).

Where colour has faded, remove the old polish with steel wool and white spirit, wash, rinse and when dry apply pigmented wax polish, such as Cardinal Red Tile Polish, sparingly and buff well to ensure that particles aren't picked up on shoes. White patches on newly laid quarry tiled floors are caused by lime in the concrete sub-floor. In time they will fade and the process can be hastened by washing down with a vinegar and water solution (60 ml or 4 tablespoons vinegar to 5 litres water). Do not rinse—leave to dry, and repeat the treatment without polishing until the patches disappear.

Rubber Wash down with a soapflake solution, rinse and allow to dry before applying emulsion polish, such as Seel self-shine floor polish. Never use synthetic detergent or solvent-based wax polish as these can soften the surface. To remove scuff marks, follow the floor maker's instructions or use a sparing application of a mild abrasive powder cleaner on a damp cloth. Rinse off quickly with clear water. Damage may occur if done too frequently.

Stone Mop or scrub when necessary with a detergent or washing soda solution (use a handful to a bucket of warm water). Floors in vulnerable areas like kitchens are best sealed with something like Bell Sealer or Bourneseal as this makes cleaning much easier. Before sealing a floor make sure that it is thoroughly cleaned and that any grease marks have been removed—try Bell 1966 Cleaner.

Vinyl (sheet and tile) Regular sweeping cuts down on the frequent necessity for more thorough cleaning. When this is necessary, damp mop with clear water adding a little general purpose cleaner if soiling is heavy. When dry apply emulsion polish, such as Johnson Klear, sparingly. Polish will build up over a period of time and should be removed with the manufacturer's recommended remover or a proprietary floor polish remover, *eg* Marley Cleaner. Solvent-based wax polish should never be used on vinyl. Scuff marks should be treated with a soft pencil rubber or a cloth dipped in emulsion polish, such as Johnson Klear, Seel.

Wood (block and strip) Always keep swept or dry mopped to keep dust and grit from becoming embedded. While a damp cloth can be used to remove sticky marks, never actually wash a wooden floor as over-wetting can seep between boards causing them to warp, or blocks to loosen. If a wax polish has built up on a wooden floor, you can remove it with a cloth and white spirit (turpentine substitute). This is flammable so don't smoke and make sure the room is well ventilated. Alternatively rub along the grain with steel wool dipped in liquid or paste wax, *eg* Johnson Beautiflor or Mansion Wax. Allow the wax to harden, then polish thoroughly. Stubborn marks can also be removed by rubbing with fine steel wool. Repolish the floor using a solvent-based polish,

Check first with safety rules on page 5

such as Mansion Wax, Johnson Beautiflor. Where a floor has been sealed with varnish or a polyurethane dressing, clean by damp mopping or an occasional application of a wax or self-shining emulsion cleaner/polish, such as Dual.

Formica *see* LAMINATED PLASTIC SURFACES.

Freezer
When a freezer has finished defrosting (to do this follow the freezer manufacturer's instructions) wash out the interior with warm water and bicarbonate of soda (15 ml bicarbonate of soda to each litre water). Do not use a detergent solution which might taint the plastic. On stains use neat bicarbonate of soda on a damp cloth.

    If a freezer has defrosted itself while still full of food due to a fault, it may smell very strongly. In this case wash out as suggested above then swab the interior with a solution of Milton Sterilizing Fluid (1 capful to 1·2 litre water). Do not use on metal sections. When the inside is dry fill the freezer with screwed-up newspaper and leave it turned off for a couple of days with the door slightly ajar—the newsprint should absorb the smells. Repeat the treatment if necessary.

Clean the outside of the freezer with a mild detergent solution, rinse and wipe dry. To protect against marks and maintain shine use an aerosol cleaner/polish such as Sparkle or Mr Sheen.

French-polished surfaces

Dust and buff along the surface of the grain regularly. Occasionally apply a coat of wax polish such as Antiquax paste wax and rub in thoroughly. Light marking and a build-up of wax can be removed with a proprietary product, such as Antiquax Spirit Cleaner, or a solution of 1 part white vinegar to 8 parts warm water applied on a well wrung-out chamois leather. Dry with a soft cloth.

If French polish looks dingy or faded treat it with Rustin's Polish Reviver applied on a soft cloth rubbed in the direction of the grain. This should also remove light scratches; more serious ones will need repairing with a home French polish such as Furniglas, following the maker's instructions. Serious damage on valuable pieces should be repaired professionally.

Fur

Natural fur needs care to keep it in condition once it is no longer on an animal's back and able to absorb natural oils. Store fur garments in a loose, closed bag of cotton or silk, hung on a well shaped, long-necked, padded hanger with plenty of space around the garments. If a fur coat is not worn regularly, give it a good shake from time to time and always shake it before you put it on. Put fur into cold storage in summer to revive it and during winter hang it in a cool room where the skin can get plenty of air.

Most coats are moth-proofed and home moth-proofing of any kind should be avoided. If a fur gets wet allow it to dry naturally. Have your fur cleaned professionally, preferably by the furrier who sold it to you. Never attempt any form of stain removal yourself. Obtain professional treatment at once if a tear or split occurs or if you see loose hairs coming out from a fur.

Fur fabric

Most fur fabrics are acrylic, acrylic mixtures or polyester crêpe, sometimes knitted and sometimes woven. The vast majority can be washed and garments made from them carry a label giving the appropriate International Textile wash care information. They should be shaken well while damp and dried naturally. If fur fabric needs dry-cleaning this should be done professionally because

Check first with safety rules on page 5

cool drying, not obtainable in coin-op machines, will be needed.

Straight pile fur fabric should be brushed while slightly damp but curly pile should never be brushed while damp. In between washing or dry cleaning, keep the pile looking attractive and tangle-free by brushing with a medium-hard brush. Do not allow fur fabric to become too soiled before cleaning.

Furniture

GENERAL CARE

You need to know what your furniture is made of before you can treat it effectively. In general there is less need than most people imagine to polish often—you cannot, after all, feed wood that is only a veneer. Many modern finishes just require wiping over with a damp cloth to keep them clean and no attempt should be made to produce a shine on a piece designed with a matt finish. Many modern pieces of furniture come supplied with a care label. Failing this, it is worth asking the retailer or manufacturer what specific care is recommended for a particular finish. It may be useful to know that you can buy specially impregnated dusters, for example Freshtex, which are designed to collect dust rather than spread it around (*see* ADDRESSES).

Specific information on cleaning certain types of furniture is given under the headings ANTIQUE FURNITURE, BAMBOO, FRENCH-POLISHED SURFACES, GARDEN FURNITURE, GLASS, LAMINATED PLASTIC SURFACES, PAINTED SURFACES, PLASTICS, ROSEWOOD, TEAK and WOOD, all in this section.

REMOVING MARKS FROM FURNITURE

Note Where furniture is antique or valuable it is best to *seek professional advice* for all these marks. For removing any marks from French-polished furniture *see* FRENCH-POLISHED SURFACES.

Alcohol stains

If alcohol stains do not respond to a good polishing, they can sometimes be removed by rubbing along the grain with metal polish or a mixture of linseed oil and cigarette ash made into a paste.

Bruise marks

May be removed by saturating a piece of blotting paper with water, folding it over several times to make a thick wad and placing over the marks. Hold a hot iron over the blotting paper, supporting its weight and taking great care that no part of the iron touches the wood. Finish by polishing as usual.

Burns

Where a burn has just caused light discolouration, rub the mark with metal polish, *eg* Brasso, working in the direction of the grain.
on waxed or oil-finished wood Rub hard over burn marks with turpentine.

On all types of wood, where a burn has roughened the surface, scrape over the rough area with a very sharp knife, taking care not to gouge out unmarked wood (hold the blade as flat as possible). Smooth over with a very fine abrasive paper. Never do this on veneered finishes. *See* DENTS, below.

With deep burn marks, scrape out the burned wood until you have a clean hole. Fill this with a matching wood filler, *eg* Brummer Stopping. Use tiny amounts of shoe polish to tint the filler if you cannot buy an exactly matching shade. Smooth the filler level with the wood surface, apply polish as usual and buff.

Dents

in solid wood Treat as soon as possible while the wood fibres are still loose. Place a little warm water in the hollow to see if the fibres swell sufficiently to raise the dent. If they don't, clean off

Check first with safety rules on page 5

the wax from the damaged section, lay a piece of damp blotting paper over the dent and apply the tip of a warm dry iron on it. When dry use a similar colour shoe polish to tone in the raised wood. Polish as usual.

in veneered wood Avoid hard rubbing or wet treatments which could damage the veneer. Dents in veneer usually split the finish so a repair is necessary. Buy a small new piece of similar veneer— an art shop that stocks marquetry sets is a good place to look. Lay the new veneer over the damaged section and with a sharp modelling knife cut an oval shape through both layers, all round the dent or split. Lift off the patch section and remove the damaged oval using a narrow wood chisel. Wet it first to soften the glue.

Dampen the new piece of veneer to make it pliable, apply wood adhesive to the back and press it into position. Wipe off the surplus adhesive before it marks the surrounding wood. After about 10 minutes, smooth the veneer down with a rounded screwdriver handle or other smooth object so that it beds in well. Leave to dry and harden overnight, then smooth over with fine abrasive paper and colour to match, if necessary, and buff.

Heat marks

These often look like a white ring. If the surface is not roughened you may be able to burnish out the mark with turpentine rubbed briskly in the direction of the grain.

Ink

Ink is difficult to remove, especially if it's an old stain. Work carefully as the method is fairly drastic and can be quickly overdone. Use a matchstick or cotton wool bud and dab the mark with a household bleach, then blot up with an old cloth or kitchen paper. Several quick dabs are better than rubbing, which will produce light spots. For a large area, or stubborn old marks, try a wood bleach, *eg* Rustin's, working carefully and following the manufacturers' instructions.

Scratches

Light scratches can often be masked using a similar coloured wax crayon or shoe polish. Apply, leave for a while, then buff briskly. Alternatively use a proprietary product such as Joy Scratch Dressing.

Water marks

First try burnishing with turpentine as for heat marks. If this fails, rub along the grain with a metal polish such as Brasso. Polish and buff. Where the surface has roughened, use very fine steel wool (000 grade) dipped in liquid wax polish. This method should be used with extreme care on veneered finishes.

COMMON PROBLEMS WITH FURNITURE

As stressed earlier, where furniture is antique or valuable it is best to *seek professional help* when problems arise. The following advice on care and maintenance refers to 'everyday', humbler furniture of various kinds.

Hinges

Hinges on cabinet furniture often become dry and stiff and if the door is forced open may distort. To cure this, drip a little oil into the top of the hinge so that it runs into the central spindle. Leave it a little time to work and then carefully open and close the door until it swings freely. For hinges that are inaccessible or very stiff use an aerosol lubricant, *eg* Rocket WD40, but hold a wad of rag around the hinge so that it doesn't get on the surrounding wood.

Sticking drawers

Drawers may stick either because the wood has swollen through

Check first with safety rules on page 5

damp or because the runners are worn. Where swelling has occurred, remove the drawer and rub soap or candle along the runners or sides. If this doesn't produce any improvement, remove the drawer and carefully smooth the runners or bottom edges with glasspaper wrapped round a wood or cork block. Rub at an angle to the edge so that you put a slight chamfer on the wood. If the runners are worn they should be replaced with hardwood strips of the correct size.

Garden furniture

Garden furniture, whether it stays out all year or goes into winter storage, needs appropriate care to keep it in condition.

Cane   For the care of cane *see* BASKETWARE AND CANE. Cane garden furniture should always be stored indoors in winter, though not in a heated place as the change of atmosphere can cause it to splinter.

Canvas   Canvas parts on garden furniture are usually rot-proof and should just be wiped over with a damp cloth from time to time. Mend any tears as they occur to prevent complete ripping apart. Canvas parts can be replaced easily as pre-cut seat and back-cover lengths are sold in shops specializing in garden furniture. Fix the canvas with domed tacks on wooden frames; wrap the ends of the canvas around metal frames and sew securely, using a darning needle and heavy twine.

Hardwood   Hardwoods like teak, cedar and iroko will withstand the roughest weather, though prolonged damp may cause discolouration. Marks can be removed with steel wool rubbed along the grain and over-all discolouration may need the application of a wood bleach—follow the maker's instructions. Treat hardwoods with an exterior grade wood preservative, such as Roncedar or Cuprinol Teak Oil. Hardwood furniture that spends the winter outside should be stood on wooden blocks to prevent the base or feet being permanently damp.

Metal   If the tubular type, keep the hinges working well with a drop of household oil. If they have become seized up, use an aerosol lubricant, such as Rocket WD40. Aluminium frame furniture just needs wiping with a damp cloth, wrung out in washing-up liquid solution, to keep it clean. Greasy marks can be removed by adding a tablespoonful of laundry borax to this solution. Corroded parts should be scrubbed with the solution, then rinsed and dried. To restore the shine rub with dry steel wool, always working in one direction to avoid scratching. When dry, dust it down and apply two coats of Joy Transparent Paint.

Tubular steel furniture usually has a rust-resistant finish but the risk of rust can be kept at bay by rubbing down with a smear of oil or grease, particularly during winter. Cast-iron and steel furniture usually has an enamel-painted finish and just needs wiping over with a damp cloth or a hose-down. Hinges will need occasional oiling and any chipped areas should be treated with a proprietary rust remover, such as Sanderson Kurust or Jenolite Rust Remover, before repainting with exterior grade enamel.

Plastic Wipe over with a damp cloth and use a mild detergent solution on dirty spots.

Softwood When new, seal wooden framed furniture by treating with a polyurethane lacquer, such as Translac Clear Polyurethane or Rustin's Clear Plastic Coating, to protect it. Dirty furniture should be scrubbed down with detergent solution, then rinsed and dried before applying the seal. Marks can be removed from the bare wood by rubbing along the grain with fine steel wool. You will need to reapply the seal each year to keep the furniture in good condition.

Gilding

Cleaning is only necessary when discolouration occurs, otherwise just dust. To clean, treat with a cloth dipped in warm turpentine or turpentine substitute. Do not heat the turpentine in a pan directly over heat but place it in a bowl of hot water as it is highly flammable.

Glass

Glass surfaces Items like glass-topped tables and glass-fronted bookcases should have the glass cleaned with window cleaner or an aerosol furniture polish; apply it sparingly then buff free of smears.

Mirrors *See* MIRRORS.

Windows *See* WINDOWS.

Oven-to-table ware Wash-up in the usual way. Stuck-on food will usually come off after soaking. Some can be put in a dishwasher.

Glasses

Wash in warm water, using your usual washing-up liquid. Rinse

Check first with safety rules on page 5

in the same temperature water, drain and dry with a soft linen cloth or chamois leather. Cotton cloths tend to leave fluff. Always wash glasses separately, using a plastic bowl or rubber mat in the sink. Do not store glasses stacked one inside the other as they may stick. Take particular care when drying stemmed glasses as the stems are easily twisted off.

Everyday tumblers can be washed in a dishwasher, but fine crystal and cut glass should always be washed by hand to avoid the 'etching' that can result from continual cleaning in a dishwasher.

Glass fibre

Baths and sinks *see* BATHS, GLASS FIBRE.

Curtains Although flame-retardant, crease-resistant, shrink- and moth-proof, glass fibre curtains split easily if they are handled a lot or undergo friction. Remove the curtain hooks and any weights and wash by hand, one at a time, squeezing gently in warm soapsuds or a mild detergent solution. Don't rub or twist. Wash them in the bath so that there is less risk of the crushing which could crack the fibres. Always wear rubber gloves as glass fibre can irritate the skin. Drip dry the curtains without folding and do not use clothes pegs. Rehang whilst still slightly damp and gently smooth out the seams and hems.

Gloss paint *see* EGGSHELL, EMULSION AND GLOSS PAINT.

Goatskin

Rugs Should be cleaned professionally as goat's hair is very brittle and can break away at the base if washed at home. Coats are specially treated to avoid this. Follow the care label's advice.

Gold

Gold articles should be cleaned with a special impregnated polishing cloth, *eg* Goddard's Long Term Silver Cloth, kept for this purpose; then buff with a chamois leather. Gold chains should be washed in a bowl of warm soapy water using a soft-bristled brush if necessary to get into the links. Rinse and allow to drip dry before rubbing over with a chamois leather. Heavily tarnished gold requires professional cleaning.

Gold leaf

No other treatment than careful dusting is required unless the gold leaf becomes discoloured. In this case dab gently with a solution of 10 ml ammonia to a cup of warm water. Rinse with clear water and dry carefully with a soft cloth. Touching up with a 'gold leaf' paint will always be noticeable.

Grasscloth
Wallcoverings made from grasscloth are difficult to clean without damaging the grasses. Use a vacuum cleaner tool to remove surface dust and do not stand furniture against them which could rub and mark them. Grease marks may never come off but it's worth doing a test with an aerosol grease solvent, *eg* Goddard's Dry Clean, to see if it will damage the grasscloth—if not, have a go but take care.

Hessian-covered walls
The dyes used in hessian wallcoverings are usually weak and not stable so the best method of cleaning is to remove embedded dust with a vacuum cleaner tool. Hessians should never be hung in a kitchen or bathroom because of the cleaning difficulties. For marks never use water or stain removers but try rubbing over them with a piece of slightly stale bread.

Horn
Use only warm water as horn can soften in high temperature water. Wash carefully in warm distilled or softened water using either soapflakes or washing-up liquid. Polish with a metal polish—the best is Solvol Autosol (from car accessory shops). Do not polish drinking vessels without washing them thoroughly afterwards.

House plants
Plants that live indoors tend to be the type that started life in the tropics. Basically their needs consist of warmth, light, air and food. Some people think they also need company and conversation but these will depend on the temperament of the owner rather than the type of plant. Plants do not need excessive heat and most will die in temperatures over 24°C (75°F). A cool spot is fine for most, but what should be avoided is constant change of temperature—for example in rooms where there is no heat by day and a coal fire at night.

Plants are more likely to thrive if they get plenty of natural daylight and will be happier in rooms where white walls and ceiling

Check first with safety rules on page 5

can help to reflect it. Artificial light, provided it is fluorescent, will also help plant growth. Some fresh air is necessary for an indoor plant to flourish and in good weather it is a good idea to stand them by an open window or door or even give them a short spell completely outside. Guard against draughts though and never give them doses of really cold air. Note that fumes from gas, solid fuel appliances and dirty oil heaters can damage house plants, as can fumes from freshly applied paint.

Food must be supplied by fertilizers once the plant has used up the supply of plant food present in the potting medium. Plants need only be fed during the growing season and should be left to rest when dormant. Many house plants from shops and nurseries come with a care-label attached and you can ask a knowledgeable seller to give you additional tips. If you want to grow a house plant successfully, it would be sensible to invest in a book giving information on what different varieties require.

Like other household items, plants will get dusty; the dust will form a film over the plant and prevent it from breathing as well as eventually spoiling its appearance. Dust can be removed by syringing or sponging the leaves with clear water. Very dirty leaves, for example on a rubber plant, should first be dusted with a soft cloth. You can buy proprietary leaf shiners which give glossy leaves back their sheen but these should only be used sparingly and occasionally. Pruning, training and repotting should be done when necessary.

Indoor plants *see* HOUSE PLANTS.

Iron, pressing
The soleplate of an iron may become marked by starch or scorching. To remove these marks, rub the iron over a damp piece of loosely woven cloth held taut on the corner of a table or ironing-board. Alternatively, use the proprietary iron cleaner Vilene Iron-cleaner. Very fine steel wool will remove bad marking but avoid scratching the soleplate and never use on a non-stick surface. When removing these marks from a steam iron, hold it in the ironing position so that the dislodged particles do not fall into the steam vents and clog them up.

Steam irons will eventually become furred-up in hard water areas though this can be considerably reduced by using demineralized or distilled water, preferably purchased from a chemist (do not use the water collected when defrosting the fridge which, although demineralized, could be contaminated). Although some models of iron require professional defurring, on others you can do the job yourself, using a proprietary scale remover such as Albright Scale Away or Descalite and following the manufacturer's instructions.

Iron, wrought

If new and without a painted finish, give decorative wrought iron used indoors a protective treatment by applying a lacquer, *eg* Rustin's Transparent Lacquer. If this produces an unpleasantly shiny result, tone it down with a light coat of wax polish. Where rust has got a hold, use a proprietary rust remover, *eg* Jenolite, following the maker's instructions.

Hinges which are corroded or rusty should be treated with penetrating oil, *eg* 3-in-1, to make them work efficiently again. Once it has penetrated, wipe the oil off, clean the area with turpentine substitute and apply a lubricant such as Rocket WD40.

Ivory

Ivory may be any colour from white to yellow. Daylight will help to maintain a good creamy colour and sunlight has a bleaching effect, but avoid strong sunlight through glass on ivory as the heat produced can cause drying and cracking. Extreme cold is dangerous too, particularly for ivory-backed hand mirrors, as the ivory can contract and crack the glass or the ivory itself.

To maintain high polish on ivory, dust it daily with a soft cloth, using a soft brush to get into the crannies on carved and intricate pieces. Antique ivory should never be put in water as after a period it will develop hair cracks even though no initial damage seems to have been done. To keep them in good condition, mirrors and brushes can occasionally be rubbed with cotton-wool dampened in methylated spirit. This cleans the ivory, maintains its polish and helps keep the surface free of the acids which cause discolouration. Valuable antique ivory should not be treated with methylated spirit.

Ivory is semi-porous and will absorb spots of toilet preparations, scent or hair spray. These should be wiped off immediately or the resultant stains may require professional attention. To wash an ivory-backed hairbrush use a warm soapflake solution on the bristles (never detergent or ammonia). Do not immerse the ivory back. Rinse the bristles in clear water, wipe the back and tap the bristles on a towel to remove as much water as possible, then

Check first with safety rules on page 5

gently dry them, facing downwards, so no damp gets into the ivory. Avoid drying them by artificial heat, such as in an airing cupboard or on a radiator, which could cause the ivory to crack.

Jade

Jade should be handled with care and any non-jewellery items dusted carefully. Fingermarks and surface soiling can be removed with a soft-bristled brush dipped in warm soapy water (don't use synthetic detergent). Rinse the item quickly in clear warm water then dry it with a soft cloth and buff with chamois leather.

Jet

Shiny jet should be buffed occasionally with a soft dry cloth or chamois leather. Dull jet should just be dusted as necessary. Never use water, polish or abrasive on either shiny or dull jet.

Jewellery

Jewellery needs care if it is to remain in perfect condition and, if real, keep its value. All good jewellery should be cleaned professionally once a year by a reputable jeweller who, to protect his reputation, cannot afford to do a bad job. This will not only clean the jewellery but ensure that it is checked for worn links, loose stones, damaged claws, *etc*. It is sensible for insurance purposes to have good jewellery revalued once a year while it is being cleaned; the value of jewellery continues to increase and inadequate insurance might mean you would be unable to replace a treasured piece.

Regular home care for jewellery is necessary to maintain sparkle. Porous stones such as turquoise and opal should never be immersed in water but just polished with a chamois leather, using a dry, soft, bristle brush to clean claw settings. Pearls, too, should never be washed. The oils from your skin will help to maintain their gleam, so wear them as much as possible (but not while applying make-up, scent or hair lacquer), and rub them gently with a chamois leather from time to time. Marcasite jewellery should also be polished with a soft brush, then rubbed gently with chamois leather and should never be washed.

Hard stones, which includes amethysts, diamonds, rubies and sapphires, can be cleaned in a warm solution of Fairy Liquid and scrubbed gently with a soft toothbrush or eyebrow brush. Rinse in lukewarm water, then dip quickly into surgical spirit to remove any remaining detergent film before draining on absorbent paper and buffing with a chamois leather. These stones can also be cleaned by immersion in a jewellery care kit, *eg* Goddard's. Gin, despite popular myth, is not a satisfactory substance for cleaning precious stones.

Certain stones require extra special care. Emeralds, for instance, are softer than the other precious stones and can chip easily. They can be cleaned in a warm solution of Fairy Liquid, as above, but care should be taken. Although diamonds are very hard, they have a grain similar to wood and a hard knock could split them. Diamonds may also scratch other diamonds if stored close together.

Always wash jewellery in a plastic bowl with an old towel or piece of absorbent cloth placed in the base. This will prevent pieces getting damaged, or disappearing down the plughole. But put the plug in—just in case.

Kettle

How you clean the exterior of your kettle, be it electric or the hob type, will depend on what metal it is made of—*see* ALUMINIUM, COPPER, ENAMELWARE, STAINLESS STEEL, *etc*. Cleaning the interior is more of a problem, as fur builds up and makes the kettle less efficient. Ideally you should deal with fur as soon as it starts to

Check first with safety rules on page 5

form rather than wait until there is a thick layer. There is a choic of descaling agents on the market, but it is important to check th kettle manufacturer's instructions to see if a particular type or bran is recommended. Descalers come in both powder and liquid form and are easy and not messy to use. Most are suitable for alu minium, brass, copper or iron, but not recommended for zinc galvanized or enamelled metal. Basically, you just add the de scaling agent to warm water in the kettle and leave it to fizz unti the scale dissolves, neutralize, then rinse out several times. Follow the maker's instructions and wear household gloves.

Knives, kitchen

Kitchen knives have either stainles steel or carbon steel blades For care of stainless steel blades *see* STAINLESS STEEL. Carbon stee blades should be washed and dried immediately after use to preven food acid stains or rust building up. Where staining has already occurred, rub the blades with a nylon scouring pad and, if this does not remove the marks, rub them with the flat end of a wet cork dipped into an abrasive cleaning powder, *eg* Vim, or use wet or dry abrasive paper. Rub vegetable oil over blades to protect them while stored. Handles tend not to be dishwasher-proof, particularly if made of wood which is likely to split. Plastic handles can usually be put in a dishwasher safely.

Lace, discoloured or yellowed

Antique lace For cotton lace that is heavily discoloured or yellowed, professional treatment should be sought since the method of bleaching required is a highly professional one. For badly discoloured silk lace, unfortunately little can be done in the way of professional treatment. *Never use any home bleaching method for either.*

Some improvement can, however, be effected by soaking antique cotton or silk lace in clear cold distilled water over a period of several hours. The lace should be laid as flat as possible on a piece of white nylon net so that it can be lifted out of the water without strain being imposed on it. Change the water several times as the discolouration starts to lift from the lace. Finally raise the lace on the net and slide it, wet, on to a smooth surface—a sheet of polythene is ideal. Make sure there is plenty of water still in it and pull it carefully to shape, then blot it well with a towel. The lace can be pinned out using rustless pins. Allow it to dry naturally in an airy place, away from direct sunlight. On no account should the lace be pressed or ironed.

Machine-made lace Today's machine-made laces are mainly man-made fibres. Discoloured nylon lace which does not respond to laundering may be improved by the careful use of a proprietary nylon whitener, *eg* Dylon Nylon White. In the case of a polyester fibre, *eg* Terylene, use Dylon CC Curtain White. Most modern curtain nets are made in a polyester fibre.

Lacquer

The term lacquer is used to describe the transparent sealing coat applied to metals such as brass or copper. It is also used for objects lacquered under the old Chinese system which should be cleaned simply by dusting.

Metal sealing lacquer also needs no care apart from routine dusting. If areas of lacquer get rubbed off or chipped, the metal will eventually start to discolour. The only remedy for this is to remove all the lacquer with a proprietary lacquer remover, *eg* Joy Takesitoff or nail polish remover (both flammable), clean the metal according to type, then re-apply a layer of lacquer.

Laminated plastic surfaces

Laminated plastic surfaces are now found all over the home, in kitchen, bathroom, bedroom and living room.

Formica and Perstorp Warerite are the tough laminates, used in areas of hard wear. These will stand up to kitchen worktop use though you should not chop directly on them nor put anything on to them straight from the cooker.

Wiping with a damp cloth will keep the surface clean and washing with hot soapy water should remove most marks. For obstinate food and ink stains, apply neat washing-up liquid or a cream cleaner, *eg* Jif, and rub gently with a damp cloth.

Melamine-faced chipboard is another plasticized surface usually used in doors, vertical surfaces and shelves. It's not as strong or durable as the laminates and is more easily stained. Clean as above.

PVC (polyvinyl chloride) surfaces are often found on self-assembly bedroom furniture. They are tough and scratch resistant but their construction—a sheet of PVC foil stuck to the solid panel with adhesive—means that if the corners become unstuck you can peel the whole sheet off. Clean with a damp, soapy cloth, but do not over-wet.

Check first with safety rules on page 5

Lampshades

Lampshades are meant to cast light in an attractive manner and they will not do this if they are allowed to collect dust and dirt. Dust lampshades regularly as part of your routine cleaning. From time to time before they begin to look soiled, clean them according to what they are made of.

Buckram A stiff brush will be needed to remove dust. Marks can be removed by rubbing the shade with a cloth dipped in turpentine. Go over the whole shade to avoid a patchy effect.

Plastics Sponge with a cloth wrung out in warm, soapy water, then in clear water. If the whole lampshade is washable immerse it and swish round in soapy water, then in clear water; pat dry with a soft cloth.

Vegetable (imitation) parchment This should never be wetted or it may disintegrate. Dust with a soft cloth or brush and rub gently at any marks with a soft, clean india rubber.

Vellum (parchment) Wipe over with a solution of 1 spoonful of soapflakes in an equal amount of water plus 2 spoonfuls of methylated spirit, shaken together. Rinse with a cloth moistened in methylated spirit. Polish with Renaissance Wax Polish (*see* ADDRESSES). *See also* VELLUM.

Lavatory

Lavatory pan Scrupulous and regular cleaning is essential to keep germs at bay. A lavatory pan should be cleaned every day by brushing around the pan with a lavatory brush followed by flushing. Keep the brush clean by regular washing in hot soapy water followed by rinsing in cold water to which you have added a few drops of disinfectant. At least once a week clean the pan with one of the powder or liquid products sold for this purpose. Do not leave either type in contact with the surface longer than recommended otherwise penetration may occur through worn areas or cracks in the glaze, resulting in discolouration.

Never use a powder lavatory cleaner with another cleaner as toxic gases could be released. If a cleaner is left in the lavatory overnight be sure to flush it in the morning before the lavatory is used. Consider using in addition to an ordinary cleaner a flush block which is sited in the cistern and contains detergent which is flushed around the lavatory after each use.

Lavatory seat Keep a special cloth for cleaning purposes and use

94

, dampened in a warm water and disinfectant solution, to wipe the lavatory seat on top and underneath every day. At least once week give the same treatment to the outside of the pedestal.

Lead

Garden ornaments Some people like the natural weathered appearance of lead and prefer to leave it without attention. It can be cleaned by scrubbing with turpentine until the desired colour is reached, then hosing down. Heavily soiled pieces may need treatment with a household scouring powder, *eg* Vim.

Leather

Leather keeps the animals whose skin it is protected from the elements. If looked after correctly, it can do the same for you and should give years of wear.

Book *see* BOOKS.

Chamois Wash by hand following the manufacturer's instructions. Where none exist, prepare a warm soapflake solution and squeeze the chamois leather in it to release the dirt. Rinse once, in warm water with 5 ml of olive oil added and swished around to disperse it. Squeeze out as much moisture as possible. Pull into shape and hang in an airy place away from artificial heat. Hand flex the leather during drying to maintain its suppleness.

Clothing Leather clothing is often described as 'washable', which in fact means 'spongeable' as it should not be immersed in water. Most clothing comes with care instructions from the manufacturer and these should be followed. All leather clothing will need professional cleaning every 3–4 years, including re-tinting and re-oiling. If it gets wet during wear, wipe with a clean cloth and allow to dry naturally. Store in a cotton cover or unsealed plastic bag in a cupboard, using a well-padded hanger.

When a leather garment is new or newly cleaned, it is sensible to apply a coating of Scotchgard Suède and Leather Protector, to protect it against weather and spills. Surface soiling can be removed from washable leathers with a soapy swab (use glycerine toilet soap or a soapflake solution, not a synthetic detergent), then wipe with a clean damp cloth before hanging to dry. As the garment gets older, an occasional application of hide food will keep it looking good.

Check first with safety rules on page 5

Desk tops Providing the leather is of the washable type it can be wiped over from time to time with a damp cloth which has been rubbed across a tablet of glycerine toilet soap or wrung out in a warm soapflake solution. While damp, apply a hide food, *eg* Connolly's Cee Bee, sparingly. Ink marks can usually be removed if sponged immediately with water; ballpoint ink is more likely to respond to milk. Antique-finish leather desk tops should just have an occasional application of hide food to clean, preserve and protect the surface against staining.

Gloves Most leather gloves are washable and special glove shampoos are available. Otherwise, use a warm soapflake solution. Wash gloves on your hands rubbing gently to remove dirt. Allow them to dry naturally and when almost dry pull them on to your hands to restore the shape. Doeskin gloves should not be rinsed as the residual soap helps keep them supple. After washing, press them between two towels to remove excess wetness, then dry naturally.

Furniture Dust leather furniture regularly and give it an occasional application of hide food to prevent cracking and help protect against stains. To freshen up the surface, remove dirt with a soft damp cloth, which has been rubbed across a tablet of glycerine toilet soap or wrung out in a soapflake solution; never use synthetic detergent which may damage the surface. Do not rinse as the residual soap will help the leather to stay supple. Finish off by wiping over with a soft damp cloth. Where leathers are specifically not 'washable' take professional advice on their care.

Luggage The natural oils will keep leather luggage in good condition at first but you will then need to apply hide food occasionally. After use, loose dirt should be brushed off the luggage and the leather wiped over with a damp cloth, which has been rubbed across a tablet of glycerine soap or wrung out in a warm soapflake solution. Finish with a cloth wrung out in clear water and pat dry. Odd marks may respond to rubbing with eucalyptus oil.

Bashed and worn suitcases can have their appearance improved by rubbing over with a solution of 10 ml vinegar, 2·5 ml ammonia and 500 ml water. When dry, rub the leather over sparingly with castor oil, then polish with a silicone furniture cream such as Enriched Min Cream.

Reptile skin This, used for shoes and handbags in general, just needs dusting. An occasional application of special reptile skin dressing, *eg* Meltonian Neutral Shoe Cream—sold in a jar—or

Connolly's Cee Bee Hide Food will keep it gleaming—always rub it in gently, in the direction in which the scales lie.

Shoes and handbags Ask about care when you buy a new pair of shoes and, if a special product is required, buy it there and then. An initial application before you wear the shoes will help provide a protective surface against dirt, wet and stains. Many recommended shoe polishes not only clean but contain soluble dyestuffs to restore faded colour and cover up scuff marks. Regular applications will keep shoes looking good and restore the natural oils that get lost during wear. Handbags don't take such a drubbing as shoes but need similar care. Take care that all polish is well rubbed into a handbag or it may come off on your clothes and, for this reason, don't choose the pigmented polishes for this purpose.

Suède clothes It is possible to buy washable suède and it is worth paying extra for this since actual laundering is possible. With new or clean suède an initial application of Scotchgard Spray for Suède and Leather prevents colour rubbing off and also provides a protective surface that can be wiped lightly with a damp cloth to remove surface soiling.

When suède does become dirty, or if rain spots don't disappear despite brushing, wipe the entire section over with a cloth well wrung out in clear cold water and allow to dry naturally. Then brush up with a wire brush and it is likely that all marks will disappear. Alternatively, there are suède cleaning cloths or blocks for this purpose, *eg* Swade Groom or Swade Aid; these are particularly useful for removing soiling along wear creases. Where this home treatment fails (and before the garment is heavily soiled), take the garment to a specialist suède cleaner who will not only clean it but restore any lost colour and oil.

Suède shoes When necessary, clean with a nailbrush dipped in warm soapy water. Don't use detergent which can damage the finish. Finish with the nailbrush dipped in cold water, but do not over-wet. Blot with a dry cloth and allow to dry naturally. Alternatively, use a proprietary product such as Miss Dylon Suède and Brushed Pigskin Cleaner, following the maker's instructions. When suède shoes get wet allow them to dry naturally, then use a rubber or nylon suède brush to remove dust and raise the nap. Fresh mud should be scraped off while still wet and soiling blotted with a damp cloth.

Check first with safety rules on page 5

Once cleaned, protect suède shoes with a protective dressing such as Swade Guard or Miss Dylon Rain and Stain Repellent. Fading can be improved with an over-all application of appropriately coloured suède dressing such as Meltonian Standard Suède Dressing.

Patent Do not allow patent leather to become excessively cold or it may crack. Dust it with a soft cloth and apply patent leather dressing from time to time. If used only infrequently, apply a thin layer of petroleum jelly all over and wipe this off before each use.

Fake Clean with a soft cloth moistened in warm soapy water— not synthetic detergent which could damage it. Rinse with clear water and buff with a soft cloth.

Light bulbs

Always switch off electricity before removing a light bulb and, if the light has been on, wait for the bulb to cool down. Hold it by the cap and carefully wipe over with a well wrung out damp cloth. Dry thoroughly with a soft cloth or duster before replacing. Never attempt to clean a bulb which is still in its socket. Fluorescent light tubes should be removed and cleaned in the same way.

Linoleum *see* FLOORS.

Marble

For the care of marble fireplaces *see* FIREPLACES. For general care of table tops and mantlepieces marble just needs to be washed over with warm soapy water, rinsed and buffed with a soft cloth. Colourless wax polish can be applied to coloured marble to give it sheen, but never to white as it can cause yellowing. Surfaces used for food preparation should never be waxed. Dirty marble can be cleaned with Bell 1967 Cleaner and polished with Bell Marble Polish. Bell also make a special cleaner (*see* ADDRESSES) for badly marked old marble, but where damage or staining is extensive professional cleaning is a better bet.

Mattresses

Spring interior Turn over or swing round to reverse head and foot once a week when new, then quarterly after a month or so. This helps the filling to settle. Use the handles and if possible get someone to help you. Every so often, brush the mattress and the base below it to remove dust and fluff. Do not use a vacuum tool for this as it may dislodge the filling. Take care not to pull out tufts or buttons. It is possible to purchase white cotton covers for protecting the mattress. These are removable for laundering.

Foam Foam mattresses with a layered construction should never be turned. Single density foam mattresses should be turned once a month. Cleaning of dust and fluff can be done with the crevice tool on a vacuum cleaner.

Melamine

Tableware can be cleaned by normal washing-up. Although the manufacturers do not recommend putting melamine tableware in a dishwasher, it is usually perfectly safe to do so. Avoid abrasive cleaners; stained cup interiors can be cleaned by using the special Melfresh cleaner or a mild solution of baby's bottle sterilizer, *eg* Milton. Staining will be considerably reduced if cups and beakers are washed as soon as possible after use. *See also* LAMINATED PLASTIC SURFACES.

Metals

Metals should be cleaned carefully to avoid abrading their surface. It is important to use the correct polish for a particular metal as metals fall into two categories—hard and soft—and polish for a hard metal such as brass will damage a soft one such as silver. If you are uncertain which metal it is, in the case of a long-neglected object, play safe and use Duraglit Wadding Silver Polish. For how to clean particular metals *see* ALUMINIUM; BRASS; BRONZE; COPPER; GOLD; PEWTER; SILVER; STAINLESS STEEL.

Mirrors

Glass Glass mirrors can be cleaned in the same way as windows (*see* GLASS), using a proprietary window cleaner according to the directions and buffing up with a soft cloth. For bathroom and kitchen mirrors it is possible to cut misting by wiping the mirror with an anti-mist product, *eg* Holts Anti Mist, obtainable at cycle and garage accessory shops. Hair spray marks can be removed with a cloth moistened in methylated spirit, followed by an application of window cleaner.

Plastic Mirriwallpaper and Melinex (mainly used commercially) both scratch easily so should be cleaned with a very soft cloth or feather duster. Occasionally wipe over gently with a damp cloth wrung out in mild detergent solution (not Melinex).

Check first with safety rules on page 5

Mother-of-pearl

Cutlery handles Because mother-of-pearl is slightly porous cutlery handles are vulnerable to acid and vinegar staining and, during washing-up, grease in the water may be absorbed and produce dark stains which cannot be removed. This cutlery should be washed in warm soapy water, separately from other items. Try not to immerse the handles.

Ornaments Clean with a paste of powdered whiting (obtainable from art shops) and water. Rub it on gently then wash off with warm soapy water. Alternatively, use Enriched Min Cream.

Tables and work-boxes When cleaning items with inlaid mother-of-pearl sections avoid the sections which should be cleaned separately with a non-abrasive polish such as a white furniture cream, *eg* Stephenson's Olde English Furniture Cream. Where the mother-of-pearl is inlaid or superimposed on papier mâché (which may well look like wood), take professional advice on cleaning. Professional attention is also essential for restoring articles that are stained or have lost their natural lustre.

Nickel

This metal tends not to be widely available today, having been replaced mainly by stainless steel and chromium plate. No special polish is available, so clean it with a proprietary silver polish, *eg* Silvo.

Non-stick surfaced cooking pans

Keep the manufacturer's care instructions when you buy a non-stick lined cooking pan and follow them. Some non-stick pans can be washed in a dishwasher and the instructions will give guidance on this. In general, hand washing-up in hot water and washing-up liquid will clean most of them although some require clear water only. Do not use steel wool, scourers or abrasive powders on a non-stick surface. Usually, wooden or plastic spoons *etc*, rather than metal, should be used with non-stick pans.

From time to time rub a non-stick surface over with a wet nylon or plastic cleaning pad or stiff sponge. This will remove the build-up of grease. Heavy food stains can be removed by boiling up a solution of 1 cup water, $\frac{1}{2}$ cup liquid bleach and 30 ml bicarbonate of soda for 5 minutes, then wash the pan as usual and grease the surface lightly to recondition it. *See also* PANS, and, for non-stick bakeware, BAKING TINS.

Nylon

Fur *see* FUR FABRIC.

Fabric *see* PART 4.

Utensils *see* PLASTICS.

Oil paintings

Because oil paintings are not covered by glass, when you dust them you will be dusting the painted surface itself. When dirt builds up to a degree that needs cleaning you should seek professional treatment if the picture is in any way valuable. For less valuable works you can buy a special picture cleaner—Winsor & Newton's Winton Picture Cleaner—from art shops and follow the maker's instructions exactly. It can be used on varnished and unvarnished pictures but will remove varnish so you will need to reapply aerosol Artists' Picture Varnish—again obtainable from art shops—when cleaning is completed. It is important to use the picture cleaner carefully and stop when colour starts to come off the picture on to the cotton-wool pad used.

Onyx

Onyx is porous and will absorb even perspiration from the hands, so it should be handled as little as possible. Dust it regularly and use a damp cloth, well wrung-out in water to remove any surface soiling. Light marks can be removed by rubbing with a cloth moistened in methylated spirit. Drinks spilled on to an onyx surface will be absorbed unless wiped up immediately and the onyx will subsequently require professional regrinding and repolishing.

Ormolu

Ormolu is bronze overlaid with gold leaf and is used as decoration on furniture. If the surface becomes dulled, clean with a swab of cotton-wool well wrung out in a solution of 10 ml cloudy ammonia in a cup of warm water. Don't let it touch any wood sections; it may be necessary to mask these with cardboard cut-outs. Rinse well with a cloth wrung out in clear water, then dry with a soft cloth. Never use metal polish or lacquer.

Oven *see* COOKERS.

Painted surfaces

Walls Dust and wash using a diluted solution of washing-up liquid. Work from the bottom upwards to avoid streaks. *See also* CEILINGS AND WALLS; EGGSHELL, EMULSION AND GLOSS PAINT.

Woodwork Light soiling can be removed with an aerosol all-purpose polish such as Mr Sheen or Johnson Sparkle. These contain a cleaner as well. Really grubby patches should be wiped with a cloth wrung out of a solution of washing-up liquid, then wiped over with clear water. Use a proprietary paintwork cleaner such as Polywash or, on stubborn, greasy marks, Flash, in solution, or Ajax Liquid. Never use an abrasive as this will dull the finish and remove some of the paint film. Lustre-finished painted wood, particularly if gilded, needs special care and gentle wiping with a weak solution of washing-up liquid.

Pans

Burnt The safest way to remove burnt food from a pan is by soaking. Fill with a solution of enzyme detergent powder in hand-hot water. Leave this to soak for a few hours then bring it to the boil. Remove the softened deposit and clean the pan according to what it is made of. Only if repeated applications of this method fail will it be necessary to use an abrasive. *See also* ALUMINIUM, COPPER, ENAMELWARE, NON-STICK SURFACED COOKING PANS and STAINLESS STEEL.

Papier mâché

Dust papier mâché items regularly. Wipe over occasionally with a cloth wrung out in soapy water, wipe with clear water and dry. Protect ornamental articles with a light application of furniture cream, *eg* Stephenson's Olde English Furniture Cream.

Patent leather *see* LEATHER.

Perspex

For general care, use washing-up liquid solution, rinse and dry thoroughly. A light application of Mr Sheen will maintain shine and help repel dust. Light scratching can be removed by buffing with a soft cloth moistened with a little Brasso or Silvo. Wipe off and buff well.

Pewter

Pewter must be cleaned regularly otherwise oxide scale develops which tarnishes the surface and has to be removed professionally.

For a soft glow on your pewter just wash it in soapy water and dry it well with a soft cloth. Any grease marks can be removed with a little methylated spirit on a cotton-wool swab before washing. For a real shine use a polish suited to pewter, *eg* Goddard's Glow, or any other good metal polish or impregnated wadding such as Duraglit, always rubbing round not across the article.

Piano keys

Ivory This can discolour with age and use. Bad discolouration will require professional scraping. On pianos which are not very valuable, however, you could try a solution of equal parts of methylated spirit and warm water applied on a well squeezed-out pad of cotton-wool, followed by buffing with a soft non-fluffy cloth. Mild discolouration will often bleach out if the piano lid is left open for the sun to shine on the keys and plenty of air to circulate. For general care, wipe the keys over with a chamois leather well wrung-out in warm water to which you have added a few drops of vinegar. Don't let water trickle between the keys; wipe dry immediately.

Plastic These will not discolour in the same way as ivory. Dust them frequently and clean with a chamois leather well wrung out in warm water to which you have added a few drops of vinegar. Wipe dry.

Picture frames

Gilt or gilded Dust regularly. If discolouration appears, rub over the frame with a cloth dipped in turpentine or turpentine substitute. Branded wax gilt, Treasure Gold, can be bought from art shops and used to touch up any damaged spots. *See also* GILDING and GOLD LEAF.

Wooden Use a little furniture cream to polish regularly and buff well.

Pillows

Foam Foam pillows have a fabric cover over them. Where a spill has stained the cover but not penetrated into the foam, the cover can be unpicked and removed for washing. The foam interior is very soft and can tear easily if handled roughly. Don't leave it exposed to

---

Check first with safety rules on page 5

light or use it until it is sewn back into its own cover. Minor marking on a foam pillow can sometimes be removed by sponging with warm soapsuds followed by sponging with clear water and mopping with a towel. Do not over-wet and dry the pillow in its cover or a pillowslip near the top of a warm airing cupboard away from direct heat.

If the foam is saturated by spillage, complete immersion may be necessary. Leave the cover on and using warm, soapy water, squeeze the pillow gently, taking care not to twist or wring it. Rinse until the water is completely clear and gently squeeze out as much water as possible. Wrap the pillow in a large towel and press out further moisture. Dry the pillow very thoroughly as described above. This may take some time but persevere until drying is complete.

Natural fibre Pillows filled with down or feathers should be aired regularly, out-of-doors in summer. They can be washed by hand but, unless you own a large spin drier, this is not recommended, as drying otherwise takes an incredibly long time. Some laundries will wash pillows for you. Do not wash pillows with worn covers or damaged seams. Pillows filled with natural fibres should not be dry cleaned as it is difficult to remove all the toxic fumes from them.

To wash a pillow by hand use either the bath or the wash tub of a top-loading washing machine. Use a soapflake or mild detergent solution. Squeeze the pillow well in the suds so that the filling is thoroughly penetrated. Rinse two or three times in warm, clear water. Squeeze out the excess water then wrap round in a spin dryer, to balance the weight, and spin for not more than 30 seconds. Do not use a tumble dryer as you could damage both the dryer and the pillow.

Finally, hang the pillow, pegged at two corners, on a line out-of-doors. Take it down and shake it occasionally, then re-peg at the other two corners. It may take several days before it is completely dry, in which case bring it in at night and rehang in the morning. Air it thoroughly in a warm place before putting it on a bed.

Synthetic fibre Pillows filled with Dacron or polyester can be washed either by hand or in a front-loading machine—a laundrette machine which is larger than a domestic model is better able to cope with the size. Follow the pillow maker's instructions for drying. Synthetic-filled pillows should not be dry-cleaned.

Plants, house *see* HOUSE PLANTS.

Plastics
Plastics are among the easiest surfaces to keep clean and in general a wipe over with a mild detergent solution followed by rinsing will do the trick. Cleaner/polish sprays like Mr Sheen and Johnson Sparkle are good for maintaining a shine on surfaces which are not used for food preparation. For more specific information on the care of different plastics, *see* ACRYLIC; LAMINATED PLASTIC SURFACES; MELAMINE; POLYSTYRENE; FLOORS, VINYL.

Polystyrene, expanded
This is usually found in the form of ceiling tiles. Dust them carefully with a duster tied over a broom head, or use the brush attachment on a vacuum cleaner. Take care not to depress the surface. In a kitchen they may be greasy, in which case sponge as necessary with a warm, mild detergent solution, avoiding pressure. Rinse with clear water and allow to dry thoroughly. Re-apply emulsion paint if desired—preferably a flame-retardant emulsion such as Timonox Flame Retardant Emulsion.

PVC (polyvinyl chloride) *see* LAMINATED PLASTIC SURFACES.

Check first with safety rules on page 5

Porcelain

Real, hard-fired porcelain is not porous so can be washed in a detergent solution. Do not immerse any pieces that have cracks or chips. Rinse in clear water and dry thoroughly.

Pottery *see* EARTHENWARE.

Quarry tiles *see* FLOORS.

Radiators

Most radiators have a painted finish—see also PAINTED SURFACES. Dust, or especially in the column type, use a vacuum cleaner tool. When necessary, wipe over with a cloth wrung out in mild detergent solution. For bad soiling use a heavy duty household cleaner such as Flash. Cover the floor below a radiator while cleaning. Rinse thoroughly and wipe dry.

Refrigerators

Inside Defrost a refrigerator as soon as ice begins to build up round the frozen food compartment. Some models have automatic defrosting and just need occasional cleaning, others have to be defrosted either by pushing a button or by switching off at the electrical socket. Follow the maker's instructions. Once all the frost has melted, empty the drip tray and wipe the frozen food compartment dry.

Every 2–3 weeks, following defrosting, the interior of the refrigerator should be cleaned as follows: Remove all the shelves and fitments. With a solution of 15 ml bicarbonate of soda to 1 litre warm water, wipe over all the inside surfaces, except for the metal sections. Dry well with a soft cloth. Wash the fitments at the sink, using a washing-up liquid solution and rinsing well before drying and replacing.

Metal sections Wipe with a cloth wrung out in clear water.

Outside Wipe over the outside with a warm detergent solution and rub dry. Occasionally apply some aerosol cleaner/polish such as Mr Sheen or Johnson Sparkle.

Rosewood

For basic care of wood *see* WOOD. Use occasional sparing applications of good quality wax furniture polish, *eg* Renaissance, Mansion, Antiquax. Do not use silicone polishes or sprays which tend to produce a sticky surface. Remove surface soiling and fingermarks by wiping over with an absorbent cloth wrung out in a warm solution of 1 part vinegar to 8 parts water, but do not over-wet. Wipe dry and repolish when the surface is completely dry so that there is no danger of sealing in moisture and creating a white bloom.

Rubber flooring *see* FLOORS.

Rush matting
Vacuum rush matting as if it were ordinary pile or cord carpet. Treat stains with a solution of warm water and washing soda; occasionally sponge or scrub over the matting with soap and warm water. Lift occasionally and vacuum up the dirt which will have fallen through any holes. Otherwise it can turn to mud when the matting is wetted.

Sheepskin

Coats Do not allow a sheepskin coat to become very soiled before sending it for professional cleaning. When new or newly cleaned, spraying with a protective solution such as Swade Guard, or Scotchgard Suède and Leather Protector, will help prevent it marking. It is best to wear a scarf to guard against soiling during wear. If the collar does become soiled, however, the wool side can be freshened up with a dry hair shampoo. Home cleaning of the skin side can be done with Swade Groom or other proprietary suède cleaners.

Rugs Provided the wool is not very long, the best treatment for a sheepskin rug is to wash it yourself at home. For an average size rug you will need 175 g soapflakes, 50 ml olive oil, 50 ml glycerine, 125 g fine oatmeal and 125 g flour—the last four ingredients are for feeding and softening the skin. Boil the soapflakes and olive oil in a pan with 1 litre water, stirring well to emulsify the oil.

Add this emulsion and the glycerine to enough water to wash the skin. The wash water temperature should be warm (about 40°C). Wash the skin well, then drain off the wash water. Do one deep rinse but do not rinse out all the soap which helps to keep the skin supple.

To dry the skin, squeeze out surplus water with your hands, then rub both sides with dry towels. Hang up to dry, bearing in mind that it will be more likely to come up in good condition if not wringing wet when hung. The best place is an outdoor clothes line on a sunny, windy day; failing this put it on a rack over the

Check first with safety rules on page 5

bath. When the skin is almost dry, rub equal quantities of flour and oatmeal into the back to make good the loss of tanning materials. When the rug is completely dry, comb or brush the wool.

Shoes

Leather *see* LEATHER, SHOES.

Plastic *see* LEATHER, FAKE.

Silk wall hangings

These should always be cleaned professionally *in situ.* Do not allow them to become too dirty before having them cleaned. To keep them in good condition avoid hanging them in direct sunlight or in any room that is damp. If they have to be stored do not fold or crease them or they will crack.

Silver and silverplate

Silver and silverplate tarnish easily through exposure to certain gases in the atmosphere. Utensils for food also tarnish through contact with the sulphur in things like egg yolk, fish, green vegetables and salt. Silver and silverplate used for eating can be washed-up in the usual way, either by hand or in a dishwasher. From time to time it will need polishing to restore the shine as will other silverware around the house.

Silver polishes come in paste, liquid, impregnated wadding and impregnated cloth forms. Some polishes are described as long-term and contain tarnish inhibitors which extend the time before repolishing is needed. Long-term polishes aren't as good at cleaning heavily tarnished silver as the non-long-term types and are best used after one of the latter has been used for the actual cleaning. There are also liquids in which articles are cleaned by immersion. They should not be used on plated pieces which have any damaged plate. *Never use dip type liquids near stainless steel* sinks and surfaces which can be stained indelibly by them.

A home-made silver polish can be produced by placing a 10 cm wide strip of aluminium foil across the base of a plastic washing-up bowl, and laying the silver on top of it. Put a handful of washing soda in the bowl and cover the silver with hot water. When the bubbling stops, rinse the silver and buff it with a soft cloth. It may be necessary to repeat the treatment when there is heavy tarnishing. Stored silver should be put in acid-free tissue paper or tarnish-proof bags (available from jewellers) and kept in an air-tight box in a dry place.

Sinks

Sinks need general care to keep their outlets working properly and specific care according to what material they are made of.

GENERAL CARE

To clear any solidified grease dissolve a handful of washing soda in 500 ml boiling water and pour it down the outlet. Never put solid matter which could block the waste pipe or drain down the sink outlet. To clear a blocked drain that does not respond to the washing soda treatment, use either a proprietary drain cleaner such as Brillo Clearway, following the maker's instructions, or use a sink cup plunger remembering to block off the overflow. Serious blockages may need treating from the U bend.

SPECIFIC CARE

Fireclay Use a cleaner recommended by the Vitreous Enamel Development Council (*see* ADDRESSES) as being suitable for general or bath cleaning. Where discolouration has occurred through the glaze wearing down, use a mild solution of household bleach.

Stainless steel Rinse regularly after each use and dry with a cloth to prevent water spots forming, especially in hard water areas. Surface soiling can be removed by rubbing with neat washing-up liquid on a damp cloth. Never use harsh abrasives or scouring pads on stainless steel. From time to time polish with a proprietary product such as Goddard's Stainless Steel Care or Catercraft Formula 9 (*see* ADDRESSES) following the manufacturer's instructions.

Vitreous enamel Clean with a product recommended by the Vitreous Enamel Development Council (*see* ADDRESSES) for general or bath cleaning. Use a plastic washing-up bowl to prevent chipping, but always make sure that no gritty particles collect underneath or they may scratch the enamel.

Sisal matting

Vacuum regularly (but not when wet or muddy) and lift occasionally so that you can sweep up the particles of dirt that have fallen through any holes. Most types of sisal matting can be cleaned (but preferably as infrequently as possible) with a dry foam carpet shampoo such as 1001 Dri-foam, but it is sensible to check with the maker of the matting before attempting this. Apply the lather gently with a soft-bristled brush or sponge. Take care never to

Check first with safety rules on page 5

over-wet the matting; securing it round the edges before shampoo-ing helps to prevent shrinkage. Always allow to dry naturally.

Stains should be removed immediately; dried marks are often irremovable. Sparing applications of carpet shampoo or aerosol stain removers as applicable are most efficient in this respect.

Slate

Dust or sweep regularly and scrub when necessary with a detergent solution followed by rinsing. Heavily soiled surfaces can be cleaned with Bell 1967 Cleaner. Grease marks can be removed with Bell Oil Stain Remover (*see* ADDRESSES). If liked, you can polish with a light application of wax polish, *eg* Ronuk Wax Polish, and buff with a soft cloth. Never polish floors which could become slippery, fireplace surrounds where heat would make the wax deposit sticky, or areas such as larder shelves where food is around. *See also* FIREPLACES, RIVEN SLATE.

Spectacles

Spectacles that aren't cleaned regularly hinder rather than help vision. Wash them frequently in warm, soapy water and dry carefully with a soft cloth. Polish the lenses daily with a tissue or soft cloth, holding the frame at the top and bottom of each lens to avoid any strain. If they become misted from cooking or spotted from rain, wipe them dry and clean by breathing on both sides of the lens and polishing with a tissue or clean handkerchief. Proprietary lens cleaners are available, but should not be used on anti-reflection coated lenses, or those treated with a surface tint.

Stainless steel

Although tough and relatively stain free, stainless steel still needs a certain amount of care. Permanent staining is caused by contact with a dip type silver cleaner; hot grease or fat splashes may produce permanent rainbow coloured marks. Mineral salts in tap water can cause a white film if stainless steel is not dried thoroughly, and prolonged contact with vinegar and other culinary acids also causes staining. A proprietary cleaner, such as Goddard's Stainless Steel Care or Catercraft Formula 9 (*see* ADDRESSES), will remove most marks with the possible exception of dip type silver cleaner and heat marks.

Pitting may occur as a result of prolonged contact with water, so never leave stainless steel saucepans or cutlery soaking over-night, or undried longer than necessary. Common salt, neat bleaches, and undissolved detergent can also cause permanent pitting. Stainless steel can be kept clean by washing, either by hand in a solution of washing-up liquid or, in the case of items like cutlery—providing they are 'dishwasher-proof'—in a dishwasher. Take care to avoid spoons 'nesting' one inside another—spread them around the cutlery basket. Occasional polishing with Goddard's Stainless Steel Care or Catercraft Formula 9 will maintain the finish. For care of stainless steel sinks *see* SINKS.

Steel

Ordinary steel requires regular cleaning and occasional burnishing with fine steel wool or a medium emery cloth, though the latter can be difficult to obtain. On ornamental articles, rub over a little furniture cream such as Min to protect them from rust. Neglected items and light rust marks can be cleaned with a wire brush or steel wool. Wear goggles to prevent particles flying in your eyes. Heavier rusting will probably need treatment with a proprietary rust remover such as Jenolite (*see* ADDRESSES).

Stone

Fireplaces *see* FIREPLACES, STONE.

Floors *see* FLOORS, STONE.

Table linen

Table linen should be laundered according to the type of fabric from which it is made.

Teak

For basic care *see* WOOD. Teak is a hard wood that on factory-finished furniture needs very little special care, apart from regular dusting. Teak products such as Johnson Teak Wood Care and Rustin's Teak Oil are available, but only need sparing and occasional use (about 2–3 times a year) to clean the surface and maintain the teak's matt gleam.

Teapots

Teapots should be washed up by hand or machine according to the material from which they are made. A small teapot spout brush can be bought to clean down the spout. When stains build up to an unacceptable level, rub pottery and china with a damp cloth dipped in salt or bicarbonate of soda then rinse thoroughly.

Alternatively treat stains with a proprietary cleaner such as Chempro T or Melfresh (but not in the case of aluminium teapots) following the manufacturer's instructions. Silver teapots should have their interiors rinsed out with either clear water or a mild washing-up solution followed by rinsing. For cleaning the outside *see* SILVER. For stains on aluminium *see* ALUMINIUM.

Terrazzo flooring *see* FLOORS, CERAMIC TILES.

Thermoplastic flooring *see* FLOORS, VINYL.

Ties
Most men's ties are in a man-made fibre from the polyester, acrylic or acetate groups, or one of the natural fibres such as silk, wool or cotton. Since it is not easy to remove isolated stains without leaving a ring mark on most of these fabrics, it is a good idea to spray new, or newly cleaned, ties with a fabric protector such as the aerosol Scotchgard Fabric Protector. (Try a test area on the back of the tie and allow it to dry first.) This will prevent spills and splashes penetrating the fibres for long enough to allow them to be wiped clear.

If stain removal becomes necessary, an impregnated stain removal pad, *eg*, Spotkleen, can be very effective on grease and wine marks and is not as likely to leave a ring mark as the liquids. When full cleaning becomes necessary, follow any guidance given on the tie label. Unless labelled 'washable', professional cleaning is advised for silk and other expensive ties since pressing can be very tricky and the dyes used may not be fast to laundering. If you have difficulty in finding a dry-cleaner who will accept ties, consult the Association of British Launderers and Cleaners (*see* ADDRESSES).

Hand washing is preferable for most types of washable ties. Use a warm mild detergent solution, *eg* Dreft or Stergene, and squeeze the tie to remove soiling. Avoid rubbing since it frays and distorts the interlining. Rinse well and use a final cold rinse for all but wool. Roll in a towel to remove excess moisture then dry naturally.

Pressing a tie Polyester and other man-made fibres may not require pressing. For other fabrics, position the tie, wrong side up, on the ironing board. Make sure that the bias cut interlining is crease free, then slip a cardboard shape or 'former' up inside the wide end of the tie so you can press without transferring the shiny

112

seam lines to the face of the tie. Silk, with the exception of tussore (wild) silk, needs a warm iron and is best pressed while still slightly and evenly damp. Wild silk should be completely dry. Most tie fabrics will scorch easily, so, if you are nervous, press over a clean dry tea towel.

Tiled surfaces

Aluminium wall tiles Wipe over with a hot solution of washing-up liquid, rinse and dry with a chamois leather. Buff up with a soft cloth.

Ceramic wall tiles Clean as aluminium wall tiles. In a shower area where lime deposits may build up, clean with white vinegar wiped on neat, left on for 10 minutes to dissolve the lime then washed off. Stubborn deposits may need an acid-based cleaner made for this purpose and obtainable from tile merchants. Grouting between tiles can be cleaned with a soft brush dipped into a

Check first with safety rules on page 5

solution of domestic bleach, but take care not to loosen it. Badly marked and damaged grout is best scraped out and re-grouted.

Floor tiles *see* FLOORS, CERAMIC, QUARRY or VINYL TILES.

Mirror wall tiles Wipe down with a chamois leather or soft absorbent cloth wrung out of a solution of 15 ml white vinegar in 500 ml warm water. For further care *see* MIRRORS.

Tin

Kitchen tinware such as roasting tins, pastry cutters, graters, *etc* should be washed immediately after use in a hot solution of washing-up liquid. Rinse, then dry (a cooling oven is a good place). Discard tin items once they become rusty. *See also* BAKING TINS.

Toilet *see* LAVATORY.

Tortoiseshell
Keep items out of direct sunlight as this tends to dry them out. Preserve the lustre with a non-abrasive polish, such as Enriched Min Cream, or use a little jeweller's rouge applied on a soft cloth and buffed well. Do not use any oily preparations as these will attract dust; avoid allowing perfume or hair spray to fall on to tortoiseshell. White marks sometimes appear on neglected tortoiseshell which has been left in the sun, exposed to heat or over-wetted. These need expert attention.

When washing a tortoiseshell-backed hair brush, smear the back with a non-abrasive polish, such as Enriched Min Cream, or patent leather dressing, such as natural-coloured Meltonian Patent Leather Dressing. Wash the bristles gently by beating into a warm soapflake solution; rinse in warm water, then in cold to stiffen. Tap on a towel to remove excess moisture and leave to dry, bristles down, on a dry towel. When dry buff the back with a soft cloth or chamois leather.

Imitation tortoiseshell is usually made from celluloid or opaque horn. It needs only dusting and an occasional wipe with a damp cloth.

Upholstery
Upholstered items rarely receive the same care as clothes although they get similar, and sometimes heavier, wear. All upholstered

items should be thoroughly dusted once a week, preferably using the soft brush attachment of a vacuum cleaner; if possible use the crevice tool for around the seat edges and other hard-to-reach sections. Once or twice a year, it is a good idea to precede this treatment by beating the furniture all over with a short cane, taking care that every area is dealt with. This loosens dust that has become embedded.

Keep items out of direct sunlight as far as possible and ensure that reversible cushions are turned over once a week to give even wear. Clean upholstery before it becomes heavily soiled, following manufacturer's care instructions wherever these are available. Loose covers should be removed and either dry-cleaned or washed carefully according to type. If washed, put them back on the piece of furniture before they are completely dry to ensure a good fit and prevent shrinkage. Complete the ironing with the covers in position; be sure to use a cool iron on foam upholstery.

Where covers cannot be removed you can either call in specialist cleaners to attend to them in your home (which is expensive) or, if suitable, clean them yourself with an upholstery shampoo such as Bissell, 1001 Dri Foam or Sabco Upholstery Shampoo, following the maker's instructions. On Dralon (acrylic) velvets use only the lather from the shampoo to prevent over-wetting, which will cause the cotton in the backing to shrink. Always work in the direction of the pile, never against it. Always, too, test home treatments on an unseen area, allowing the section to dry completely for inspection before deciding to proceed.

Unless labelled 'washable', chenilles, tapestries, velours, velvets and fabrics containing silk, wool or viscose should be dry-cleaned.

Vinyl and plastic upholstery just need dusting with a soft-bristled brush and wiping with a damp cloth. More thorough cleaning can be done with a cloth wrung out in a warm solution of soapflakes followed by clear water. Alternatively use a vinyl upholstery cleaner designed for car seats, such as Turtle Upholstery Cleaner. Don't over-wet the surface.

Leather upholstery *see* LEATHER, FURNITURE.

Vellum

Remove loose dust with a feather duster or soft cloth. Wash carefully with swabs of cotton-wool wrung out in warm water, taking care not to over-wet. Wipe over with cotton-wool wrung out in milk and leave this to dry on the surface or polish with Renaissance Wax Polish. Never use a leather preservative.

Velour

Velour is expensive and difficult to produce. It should be dusted from time to time with the soft brush attachment of a vacuum cleaner and any cleaning should be carried out professionally. Home cleaning is not advisable unless it is one of the new spongeable varieties.

Velvet

Velvet may be made of silk, cotton or man-made fibres. All should be dry-cleaned unless their instructions specifically state that they can be washed. Washable velvets can usually be washed in a machine and in some cases tumble-dried. Non-washable velvets should be dry-cleaned professionally. Acrylic velvet, such as Dralon, should be cleaned using only the lather of an upholstery shampoo to avoid overwetting the backing which might shrink due to the cotton content. Alternatively it can be dry-cleaned but tell the cleaner it is acrylic and therefore a process involving strong heat should be avoided.

Vinyl

Miscellaneous Raincoats, bags, shower curtains and roller blinds should be cleaned by wiping over with a mild detergent solution and avoiding the use of abrasives.

Sheet and tile flooring *see* FLOORS, VINYL.

Upholstery *see* UPHOLSTERY, VINYL AND PLASTIC.

Wallcovering Wash with a mild detergent solution, working in an upward direction. Rinse with clear water. Do not over-wet. Work from the bottom upwards.

Vitreous enamel

Sometimes referred to as Vitramel. *See* ENAMEL, ENAMELWARE.

Warerite (Perstorp Warerite) *see* LAMINATED PLASTIC SURFACES.

Wallpaper

Ordinary wallpaper needs careful cleaning or you may damage the surface. Dust it with a soft brush or vacuum cleaner attachment, but take care not to press hard on embossed papers or you may spoil the pattern. Rubbing with a soft india rubber or slightly stale bread may prove effective on small soiled areas, such as around light switches. Never wash paper or the colours may run and the paper become loosened from the wall.

Washable wallpaper can be sponged lightly with a mild detergent solution, then rinsed using a cloth well wrung out in clear warm water. Work from the bottom upwards.

Walls *see* CEILINGS AND WALLS; EGGSHELL, EMULSION AND GLOSS PAINT; GRASSCLOTH; HESSIAN-COVERED WALLS; SILK WALL HANGINGS; TILED SURFACES; VINYL, WALLCOVERING; WALLPAPER; WOOD, PANELLING.

Wicker *see* BASKETWARE AND CANE.

Windows
Windows need cleaning both inside and out if they are to transmit light and possibly a view. Cleaning is best done on a sunless day otherwise the glass dries too quickly leaving smears. Proprietary window cleaners such as Windolene come in both liquid and aerosol form. The latter is more expensive but may be easier to apply to small areas like leaded lights.

Check first with safety rules on page 5

Home cleaners include a bucketful of warm water with 7 × 15 ml laundry borax dissolved in it, or a small bucket of water plus 30 ml vinegar. A clean chamois leather is the most effective applicator. For a really good shine, buff the dry window with a crumpled pad of newspaper—the printers' ink does a good job. Alternatively rub up with a dry chamois leather or soft cloth. A window cleaner incorporating a rubber blade is a quick way of removing the water plus dirt on large pane windows. Wipe the blade after each downward stroke.

Wood

Floors For care of both block and strip wood floors *see* FLOORS, WOOD.

Furniture For care of antique furniture *see* ANTIQUE FURNITURE. Modern furniture may be finished with French polish (*see* FRENCH-POLISHED SURFACES), oil, paint, seal or wax.
Oiled natural wood This needs little care other than regular dusting and a sparing application of a proprietary oil about 3 times a year (*see also* ROSEWOOD and TEAK).
Sealed wood Apart from dusting, just needs wiping over with a damp cloth plus an occasional application of wax furniture polish when the shine starts to disappear.
Waxed furniture Should be dusted frequently and waxed and polished thoroughly from time to time, either with a proprietary product such as Antiquax or with a home-made polish (for recipe *see* ANTIQUE FURNITURE). Be sure to apply the polish sparingly and rub really well so that a smooth patina, rather than a sticky build-up that attracts dust, is created. Fingermarks can usually be removed by rubbing briskly with a soft cloth or by wiping the surface with a cloth wrung out in a 1 : 8 solution of vinegar and warm water. Don't over-wet and dry off well.

Panelling Remove dust regularly, using a brush attachment on the vacuum cleaner or long-handled brush with a duster tied over the head.
Sealed wood panelling General cleaning is best done with a cloth wrung out in a warm, mild detergent solution. Finish with clear water and buff dry. From time to time brighten the surface with an all-purpose cleaner/polish such as Mr Sheen or Johnson Sparkle.
Wax finished panelling This needs occasional polishing with a paste wax such as Antiquax. When the wax builds up to an unacceptable, dust-attracting level, remove it with white spirit or

Antiquax Spirit Cleaner applied on a soft cloth and repolish. Neglected panelling which is faded or scratched will be improved by rubbing over with fine steel wool dipped in white spirit, working always in the direction of the grain. Then polish and buff with a soft cloth.

Utensils Wooden cheese and bread boards should be wiped over with a cloth wrung out in clear warm water and left to dry naturally in an airy place, standing on one edge so both large surfaces are exposed to the air.

Salad bowls should never be immersed in water but wiped out with absorbent kitchen paper and then with a cloth wrung out of clear warm water. From time to time apply a thin layer of corn oil to the wood and wipe it off thoroughly with kitchen paper. This type does not go rancid and helps to protect the wood against staining and maintains its sheen.

Stains can often be removed by rubbing with a nylon scourer moistened in warm water along the grain. Bad marks may need to be rubbed with wet or dry abrasive paper. Wipe the wood first with a dry cloth to remove loose particles, then with a damp one.

Pastry boards, chopping blocks, rolling pins and wooden spoons should be washed quickly and dried so that water does not penetrate the wood and cause stains. Never soak wooden utensils. Use a firm-bristled brush and scrub in the direction of the grain to remove any food particles.

Zinc
Wash when necessary in hot soapy water. Perforated zinc, such as that found on the front of old-fashioned meat safes, should be scrubbed with warm soapy water and a soft brush, then rinsed and dried thoroughly.

| Symbol | Washing temperature | | Agitation | Rinse |
	Machine	Hand		
1 / 95°	very hot (95°C) to boil	hand hot 50°C or boil	maximum	normal
2 / 60°	hot 60°C	hand hot 50°C	maximum	normal
3 / 60°	hot 60°C	hand hot 50°C	medium	cold to minimize creasing
4 / 50°	hand hot 50°C	hand hot 50°C	medium	cold to minimize creasing
5 / 40°	warm 40°C	warm 40°C	medium	normal
6 / 40°	warm 40°C	warm 40°C	minimum	cold to minimize creasing
7 / 40°	warm 40°C	warm 40°C	minimum do not rub	normal
8 / 30°	cool 30°C	cool 30°C	minimum	cold to minimize creasing
9 / 95°	very hot (95°C) to boil	hand hot 50°C or boil	maximum	cold to minimize creasing
(hand symbol)	**Do not machine wash** (the appropriate hand washing instructions are usually given alongside this symbol)			
(crossed-out symbol)	**Do not wash** at all			

Spinning/ Wringing	Fabric
normal	Used for white cotton and linen articles without special finishes, this process provides the most vigorous washing conditions. Wash temperature can be up to boiling (100°C) and agitation and spinning times are maximum. Ensures good whiteness and stain removal.
normal	For cotton, linen or viscose (rayon) articles without special finishes where colours are fast at 60°C. Provides vigorous wash conditions but at a temperature which maintains fast colours.
short spin or drip dry	For white nylon or white polyester/cotton mixtures; less vigorous than either 1 or 2. The wash temperature (60°C) is high enough to prolong whiteness, and cold rinsing followed by short spinning minimizes creases.
short spin or drip dry	For coloured nylon; polyester; cotton and viscose (rayon) articles with special finishes; acrylic/cotton mixtures; coloured polyester/cotton mixtures. Except for washing temperature identical to process 3. The lower, hand hot temperature (50°C) safeguards the colour and finish.
normal	For cotton, linen or viscose (rayon) articles where colours are fast at 40°C, but not at 60°C, this process has warm wash (40°C), medium agitation, normal spinning or wringing. The low wash temperature is essential to safeguard colour fastness.
short spin do not hand wring	For those articles which require low temperature washing, (40°C) minimum agitation, a cold rinse and a short spin *eg* acrylics; acetate and triacetate, including mixtures with wool; polyester/wool blends. These conditions preserve colour and shape and minimize creasing.
normal spin do not hand wring	For wool, including blankets, and wool mixtures with cotton or viscose (rayon); silk, which needs low temperature washing (40°C) and minimum agitation but requires normal spinning. Washing in this way preserves colour, size and handle. Do not hand wring or rub.
short spin do not hand wring	For silk and printed acetate fabrics, with colours which are not fast at 40°C, requiring to be washed at a very low temperature (30°C), with minimum agitation and spinning. Unlikely to appear on UK produced goods.
drip dry	For cotton articles with special finishes which benefit from a high temperature (95°C) wash but require drip drying. Again rarely to be found on UK produced goods.

WASHING TEMPERATURES

00°C	Boil	Self-explanatory	50°C	Hand-hot	As hot as the hands can bear.
95°C	Very hot	Water heated to near boiling temperature.	40°C	Warm	Pleasantly warm to the hand.
60°C	Hot	Hotter than the hand can bear. The temperature of water coming from many domestic hot taps.	30°C	Cool	Feels cool to the touch.

BLEACHING

 This symbol indicates that household (chlorine) bleach could be used. Care must be taken to follow the manufacturer's instructions.

 When this symbol appears on a label household bleach must *not* be used.

IRONING

The number of dots in the ironing symbol indicates the correct temperature setting—the fewer the dots the cooler the iron setting.

cool

warm

hot

do not iron

DRY CLEANING

The letter in the circle refers to the solvent which may be used in the dry-cleaning process, and those using 'coin op' dry-cleaning should check that the cleaning symbol shown on the label is the same as that in the instructions given on the front of the machine.

 Goods normal for dry-cleaning in all solvents.

 Goods normal for dry-cleaning in perchloroethylene, white spirit, Solvent 113 and Solvent 11.

 May be dry-cleaned professionally. Do not 'coin op' clean.

 Goods normal for dry-cleaning in white spirit or Solvent 113.

 Do not dry-clean.

DRYING

Care labels may also include one or other of the following symbols recommending a particular drying method.

 Tumble drying beneficial but not essential.

 Line dry.

 Drip dry: for best results hang while wet.

 Dry Flat: do not hang to dry.

IDENTIFYING MAN-MADE FIBRES

Fibre Brand Names	Man-made Fibre Group	Fibre Brand Names	Man-made Fibre Group
Celesta Dicel	ACETATE	Dacron Diolen Fortrel Lirelle Terlenka Terylene Trevira	POLYESTER
Acrilan Courtelle Dralon Orlon	ACRYLIC		
Lycra Spanzelle	ELASTANE	Cournova Meraklon Spunstron	POLYPROPYLENE
Lurex	METALLIC	Arnel Rhonel Tricel Tricelon	TRIACETATE
Acrilan SEF Kanekalon Teklan	MODACRYLIC (flame-resist-ant properties)		
Avril Vincel Zantrel Zaryl	MODAL	Delustra Evlan Sarille Viloft	VISCOSE
Antron Bri-nylon Cantrece Celon Celon Anti-Stat Counter-stat Cumuloft Enkacomfort Enkacrepe Enkalon Enkasheer Enkastat Miralon Pavanne Qiana	NYLON (POLYAMIDE)		

Note Some items of clothing and household articles/textiles may carry a fibre content label indicating the fibre group, *eg* acetate, nylon, instead of the brand name of the fibre.

Addresses

Some specialized products mentioned in the text are listed below, with indications of where to obtain them.

Albright Scale Away Hardware stores.

Antiquax Antique shops or hardware stores. In case of difficulty, write to: James Briggs Ltd., Lion Works, Old Market Street, Blackley, Manchester M9.

Bell's 1966 Cleaner (1967) A. Bell & Company Limited, Kingsthorpe Works, Northampton.

Bell Marble Polish As above.

Bell Marble 'Touch Up' Pack As above.

Bell Oil Stain Remover As above.

Bell Special Marble Cleaner As above.

Bissell Carpet Shampoo Large department stores, large hardware stores and branches of Timothy Whites.

Bissell Upholstery Kit As above.

Bourneseal Apply to Customer Services Department, Reckitt & Colman Ltd., (Industrial Division), Bourne House, P.O. Box 20, Cressex Industrial Estate, High Wycombe, Bucks, for a local representative to call.

Brasso Solvent Reckitt & Colman Limited, Reckitt House, Stoneferry Road, Hull, N. Humberside, HU8 8DD.

Brillo Clearway Hardware shops and chemists which hold a part 2 Poisons Licence.

Brummer Stopping Small DIY shops and handyman shops.

Catercraft Formula 9 Catercraft Limited, 18 Old Mill Square, Storrington, Sussex.

Chempro T Most branches of Boots and Timothy Whites.

Cleen-o-Pine Supermarkets.

Connolly's Cee Bee Hide Food Good leather shops.

Copydex Remover Copydex Limited, 1 Torquay Street, Harrow Road, London, W2 5EL.

Cuprinol Teak Oil From stockists of Cuprinol products, such as DIY shops. If no local stockist contact Cuprinol direct at the following address: Cuprinol Limited, Adderwell, Frome, Somerset.

Descalite Hardware stores.

Dylon CC Curtain White Haberdashers, haberdashery sections of department stores, some hardware stores.

Dylon Nylon White As above.

Enriched Min Cream Grocers, hardware stores, hardware sections of department stores.

Fabsil Silicone Waterproofer Scout Shops Limited (most branches). In case of difficulty, write to: Scout Shops Limited, Churchill Industrial Estate, Lancing, Sussex, BN1 8UG.

Fortificuir Alfred Maltby & Son Ltd., 28 & 30 St. Michael's Street, Oxford, OX1 2EB.

Fungo Dax Products Limited, 76 Cyprus Road, Nottingham.

French chalk Most branches of Boots.

Freshtex Most grocery outlets and Tesco stores.

Fuller's Earth Most branches of Boots.

Furniglas products DIY shops and hardware stores.

Goddard's Cabinet Maker's Wax Most hardware stores; department stores in hardware section.

Goddard's Jewellery Care Kit Jewellery sections of department stores, jewellers, silversmiths and some hardware stores.

Goddard's Long Term Silver Cloth As above.

Goddard's Stainless Steel Care As above.

Gumption Bathroom Cream Cleanser Supermarkets.